FAST CLOSE

FAST CLOSE
A Guide to Closing the Books Quickly

Second Edition

Steven M. Bragg

WILEY

John Wiley & Sons, Inc.

For general information on our other products and services, or technical support, please contact our Customer Care Department within the United States at 800-762-2974, outside the United States at 317-572-3993 or fax 317-572-4002.

Wiley also publishes its books in a variety of electronic formats. Some content that appears in print may not be available in electronic books.

For more information about Wiley products, visit our web site at www.wiley.com.

Library of Congress Cataloging-in-Publication Data:

Bragg, Steven M.
  Fast close : a guide to closing the books quickly / Steven M. Bragg.—2nd ed.
    p. cm.
  Includes index.
  ISBN 978-0-470-46501-1 (cloth)
  1. Controllership—Handbooks, manuals, etc. 2. Financial statements—Handbooks, manuals, etc. 3. Bookkeeping—Handbooks, manuals, etc. 4. Corporations—Accounting—Handbooks, manuals, etc. I. Title.
  HG4027.3.B733 2009
  657'.2—dc22
                                                                2008054909

Printed in the United States of America

10 9 8 7 6 5 4 3 2 1

To Richard Souders,
who always operates at warp speed.

About the Author

Steven Bragg, CPA, CMA, CIA, CPIM, has been the chief financial officer or controller of four companies, as well as a consulting manager at Ernst & Young and auditor at Deloitte & Touche. He received a Master's degree in finance from Bentley College, an MBA from Babson College, and a Bachelor's degree in Economics from the University of Maine. He has been the two-time president of the Colorado Mountain Club, is an avid alpine skier and mountain biker, and is a certified master diver. Mr. Bragg resides in Centennial, Colorado. He has published the following books with John Wiley & Sons:

Accounting and Finance for Your Small Business

Accounting Best Practices

Accounting for Payroll

Billing and Collections Best Practices

Business Ratios and Formulas

Controller's Guide to Costing

Controller's Guide to Planning and Controlling Operations

Controller's Guide: Roles and Responsibilities for the New Controller

Controllership

Cost Accounting

Design and Maintenance of Accounting Manuals

Essentials of Payroll

Fast Close

Financial Analysis

GAAP Implementation Guide

Inventory Accounting

Inventory Best Practices

Just-in-Time Accounting

Managing Explosive Corporate Growth

Mergers and Acquisitions

Outsourcing

Payroll Best Practices

Revenue Recognition

Sales and Operations for Your Small Business

The Controller's Function

The New CFO Financial Leadership Manual

The Ultimate Accountants' Reference

Throughput Accounting

Also:

Advanced Accounting Systems (Institute of Internal Auditors)

Run the Rockies (CMC Press)

Contents

Preface

One of the most common challenges for the controller is to close the month-end books and issue financial statements as fast as possible. The resulting statements are being demanded by corporate management, outside investors, and the Securities and Exchange Commission (SEC) (for public companies) on the shortest possible timelines. However, the closing process has traditionally been a slow one—several surveys reveal that the average company requires about two weeks to close its subsidiary's books, followed by roughly another three weeks to roll up the results into corporate-level financial statements. Companies with more organized closing systems can reduce this process to about two weeks, and those companies with the best closing processes can reduce the entire interval to four days. These results represent a slight improvement in closing times over the past—few years, but there is no massive improvement trend. Thus, companies are clearly having a difficult time shortening the closing process.

This book walks the reader through the process of closing the books and creating financial statements faster much faster. The author uses the principles outlined in this book to issue financial statements for a multidivision company in one day and has been doing so for years. Some of the key improvement steps discussed in this book are:

- Shift the timing of closing activities out of the core closing period.
- Reduce the contents of the financial statements.
- Standardize and automate the use of journal entries.
- Standardize the chart of accounts.
- Centralize accounting functions.

- Adopt inventory tracking and cycle counting systems.
- Shift rebillable expense invoices out of the core closing period.
- Use a web-based timekeeping system for consulting staff.
- Streamline the commission calculation process.
- Optimize the approval process for accounts payable.
- Link supplier invoice accruals to the purchase order database.
- Layer consolidation software onto the existing accounting software.
- Integrate an ongoing improvement review into the closing process.

These bullet points are only a microcosm of the large array of changes recommended in this book. No single change will achieve a massive reduction in the closing interval. Instead, only by gradually working through the changes listed here, in the order presented within the following chapters, can one expect to arrive at a closing interval that may encompass as little as a single day.

This second edition of *Fast Close* includes two new chapters that address critical considerations in the closing process. Chapter 14 describes the lengthy and tortuous additional steps that a publicly held company must endure while it converts its financial statements into a quarterly or annual report that must be submitted to the Securities and Exchange Commission. The chapter notes a variety of techniques for compressing these additional activities. Chapter 15 describes a number of controls over the accuracy of the financial statements. This is a particularly important issue for controllers who want to ensure that there is sufficient documentation and transactional verification to reduce the risk of issuing misleading financial statements.

This enhanced second edition of *Fast Close* is the best possible guidebook for issuing accurate financial statements within the minimum possible time period. Enjoy the journey!

STEVEN M. BRAGG
Centennial, Colorado
April 2009

1

Introduction

Achieving a fast close is a process improvement project that requires the full attention of the accounting staff for a long period of time. Before committing to such a project, one should be clear about what type of financial close works best for a company's specific needs, what kinds of benefits will result, and the general steps required to complete the close. This chapter provides answers to these questions.

DIFFERENT TYPES OF FAST CLOSE

Several variations on the fast close concept have appeared, causing some confusion about the nature of each one. The *fast close* is simply an acceleration of the standard closing process, resulting in approximately the same financial reporting package being issued (possibly somewhat stripped down). The focus of this approach is a careful examination of the closing process to strip out wait times, consolidate tasks, eliminate unnecessary functions, add transaction best practices, and selectively apply automation where necessary. It is a task in which an industrial engineer trained in efficiency improvements would feel quite at home.

The *soft close* is less labor intensive than a regular close, because it does not generate as much information. It is designed solely for internal corporate use, so its end product is only those management reports needed to run operations. With this reduced reporting goal in mind, the accounting staff can eliminate the use of overhead allocations. It may also be possible to stop some accruals and ignore the elimination of intercompany transactions, depending on the level of reporting detail desired. The soft close is most commonly seen in companies that issue only quarterly or annual reports to outside entities, leaving all other months available for the soft close.

The *virtual close* involves the use of a largely automated accounting system, one that can produce required financial information at any time, on demand. This approach is rarely used and only in the largest companies that can afford to install an enterprise resources planning (ERP) system that automatically consolidates and reports financial information. Also, the

1

underlying transactions that feed into the ERP system must be essentially error free, so an accurate virtual close is really the result of a hefty software investment as well as years of continual process improvements. The financial reports resulting from a virtual close tend to be stripped-down versions of generally accepted accounting principles (GAAP)-compliant reports, because this approach avoids the need for such manual tasks as overhead allocation, accrual transactions, and the establishment of various reserves.

If achieved, a virtual close can be useful in fast-moving industries where financial results must be monitored frequently in order to make rapid-fire changes to a company's tactical or strategic direction, or at least to identify problem areas for fast management attention.

BENEFITS OF THE FAST CLOSE

There are numerous benefits to achieving a fast close, which vary based on the perspective of the recipient—company management, outside investors, auditors, and the accounting department. These benefits are:

- *Quicker access to financial information.* Company management generally feels that the primary benefit of the fast close is having access to financial information more quickly, allowing it to take rapid steps to improve a company's strategic and tactical position in the marketplace.

- *Marketing tool.* A company's marketing staff can use the rapid issuance of financial information to trumpet the company's openness to the investing public. This does not necessarily mean that the company will issue sterling financial results, only that it will issue results faster. Still, it implies some level of expertise on the part of the accounting department in processing transactions and compiling them into reports, and so may impart some level of comfort to investors in that regard.

- *More time for financial analysis.* Closing the books fast does not necessarily mean that one must issue financial statements sooner. An alternative is to spend additional time analyzing the preliminary financial statements in order to issue more complete notes alongside the financials at a later date.

- *Improved processes.* Because the fast close improvement process requires careful attention to process enhancement, there will inevitably be side-benefit improvements to many accounting processes, leading to heightened efficiency and fewer errors. Within the accounting department, this may be seen as the top benefit of the fast close. A variety of controls for financial reporting are discussed in Chapter 15.

- *Improved control systems.* Internal and external auditors appreciate the enhanced attention to control systems needed to ensure that information is compiled properly and fast.

- *More time, period.* Although some aspects of the fast close simply push activities into the period either before or after the core closing period, some actions are completely eliminated or at least reduced in size. This results in less total time required for the closing process, which can be used by the accounting staff for a variety of other activities.

Consequently, the wide array of fast close benefits results in multiple supporting constituencies—management, investors, auditors, and the accounting department.

LEGAL ISSUES IMPACTING THE FAST CLOSE

The Sarbanes-Oxley Act has made it more difficult to achieve a fast close. The problem is Section 302 of the Act, which requires formal management certification of the accuracy of the financial statements. Specifically, Section 302 requires that the financial statements of publicly held companies not contain any material untrue statements or material omissions or be considered misleading. Understandably, those signing this certification want to spend more time ensuring that the financial statements are indeed correct. Some recent surveys of the time needed to produce financial statements have indicated a slight *increase* in the time required since the passage of Sarbanes-Oxley, probably because of Section 302.

However, Section 409 of Sarbanes-Oxley requires that public companies disclose to the public on Form 8K any information on material changes in their financial condition or operations. This must happen within four days of the occurrence of a triggering event. This requirement calls for financial and operating systems that bring issues to the attention of management faster than might previously have been the case.

Finally, the Securities and Exchange Commission (SEC) has accelerated its requirement for the timely filing of quarterly and annual reports by publicly held companies. The rule change calls for a three-year decline in the reporting period to 60 days for annual reports and to 35 days for quarterly reports (down from 90 days and 45 days, respectively). This rule applies to domestic companies having a public float of at least $75 million and that have previously filed at least one annual report.

In short, corporate controllers and chief financial officers are caught between a rock and a hard place—they must file financial and operating information sooner but want to retain it in-house longer to ensure that it is correct. The solution is still the fast close—information is available quicker for filing requirements, while company management can still retain it for further review until the accelerated filing dates come due.

STEPS TO ACHIEVE A FAST CLOSE

Several steps are required to achieve a fast close, which are addressed in detail in the following chapters. They are listed in the following recommended order of implementation:

1. *Reviewing the closing process (Chapter 3).* The first step in achieving a fast close is to examine the current state of the closing process and determine the time required to complete each functional area (i.e., inventory, billing, payroll, payables, and cash processing, as well as final closing activities). It is useful to summarize the results of this investigation into a timeline that can be used to spot which segments of the closing process are particularly in need of improvement.

2. *Altering the timing of closing activities (Chapter 4).* A set of changes that are easy to implement and yet have a startling positive impact on the duration of the close is to shift many of the closing activities either into the preceding month or into the period immediately following the issuance of financial statements.

3. *Revising the contents of the financial statements (Chapter 5).* The close will take less time if there is less information to report. There are several variations on this concept, such as eliminating custom reports entirely, shifting to electronic modes of report delivery, and reporting some operating or metric information separately from the financial statements.

4. *Optimizing the use of journal entries and chart of accounts (Chapter 6).* Journal entries require excessive amounts of time, may be entered incorrectly, and do not always contribute to the accuracy of the financial statements. Thus, standardizing journal entries, eliminating inconsequential ones, and automating them can be of considerable assistance. Also, using a common chart of accounts or at least creating mapping tables will reduce the labor associated with consolidating results reported by subsidiaries.

5. *Standardization and centralization (Chapter 7).* If a company has multiple locations, the closing process will be nearly impossible to improve unless the controller pays considerable attention to the standardization of accounting transactions so that they are completed in exactly the same way in all locations. Even greater closing improvements can be attained by centralizing accounting functions for the entire company in a single location.

6. *Closing the inventory function (Chapter 8).* The topic of inventory makes many controllers shudder, because a combination of poor controls and large investments in this area makes the cost of goods sold an extremely difficult area to calculate, leading to massive time requirements during

the closing process. This problem can be reduced by implementing tight inventory tracking and cycle counting systems, as well as by adopting better materials management policies to reduce the overall level of inventory investment.

7. *Closing the billing function (Chapter 9).* Generating month-end invoices may be the bottleneck operation during the month-end close. This problem can be reduced by shifting recurring invoices and the rebilling of expenses out of the closing period, electronically linking the shipping database to the accounting department, and ensuring fast completion of billable hours reporting.

8. *Closing the payroll function (Chapter 10).* The payroll function principally interferes with the closing process because employees are late in recording their billable hours, which can be resolved through the use of automated time clocks and Web-based time recording systems. There are also several ways to streamline the commission calculation process so it takes much less time during the core closing period.

9. *Closing the payables function (Chapter 11).* Waiting for late supplier invoices to arrive, as well as pushing those invoices through a Byzantine approval process can seriously interfere with the month-end close. There are several approaches for streamlining the basic approval process, while the intelligent use of expense accruals, coupled with the purchase order database, can eliminate the wait for late invoices.

10. *Closing the cash processing function (Chapter 12).* Some controllers like to wait until the bank statement arrives in the mail before issuing financial statements, so they can first conduct a bank reconciliation. The postal float on the bank statement can be two or three days, which directly delays the issuance of financial statements. This can be avoided through the use of online bank reconciliations, while several techniques are available for improving the speed of processing incoming checks.

11. *Incorporating automation into the closing process (Chapter 13).* There are several ways to use automation to improve the closing process, ranging from a series of small efficiency-related improvements to workflow management software, a data warehouse, consolidation software, and an ERP system.

12. *Ongoing improvements in the closing process (Chapter 16).* Although the preceding action items may have achieved a considerable improvement in the speed of the close, there is always room for improvement. Consequently, constant attention to the process flow and measurement of key metrics will ensure that the fast close remains fast.

There are two other chapters that do not have a direct bearing on speed of issuing financial statements. Chapter 14 uses many of the techniques described in previous chapters to compress the separate report filing process required of public companies by the Securities and Exchange Commission. Also, Chapter 15 describes an array of controls over the financial statement reporting process. Many of these controls can *increase* the duration of the closing process, but are critical for ensuring the ultimate accuracy of the financial reports.

The order in which improvements are listed here (and throughout the book) is intended to focus attention on low-cost, easy-to-implement changes that have a major and immediate impact on the speed of the close. Despite requiring considerable long-term effort, inventory-related changes are listed relatively high in the priority list, because the accounting staff needs to begin work on them as soon as possible in order to achieve any benefits within a reasonable timeframe. Automation improvements are listed near the bottom of the priorities, because they are generally very expensive, require considerable time to implement, and do not have a major impact on the duration of the closing process.

SUMMARY

Although the soft close and virtual close are available as alternatives to the fast close, most companies need to issue full-scale financial statements every month, which precludes the soft close. The virtual close requires considerable resources to achieve, and so is also not an option in most cases. Consequently, the focus throughout the remainder of this book is on the standard fast close, which presents considerable benefits to the implementing company.

The next chapter outlines the primary traditional closing steps required for a small single-location company, and then goes on to cover additional closing requirements for companies having multiple locations, international locations, and public reporting requirements. This information serves as a basis for the closing enhancement activities that begin to be addressed in Chapter 3.

2

Your Current Closing Process

Historically, controllers dread the first business day of the month. This is the beginning of a harrowing process that can last for weeks, as they struggle through the dozens of steps required to close the books for the preceding month. If there is an unusual result at the end of this morass, senior management may very well tell the controllers to go back and try again, in which case they are still closing the books when the *next* month is completed, which throws them into the difficult position of perpetually being in the business of closing the books—and nothing else.

This chapter covers the basic tasks required to close the books, as well as the reasons why the closing process can be so excruciatingly tangled and difficult to complete.

TRADITIONAL CLOSING PROCESS: BASIC

Company managers usually want to see financial results for every month of the year, so there is a basic closing process for each of the 12 months. On top of that, public companies create more substantial quarterly financial reports for their Form 10-Q submissions to the SEC and extremely thorough ones for their annual Form 10-K submissions. Also, multidivision companies require additional steps to consolidate financials at the division level and at the corporate level. Furthermore, international companies must convert their financial statements into a single reporting currency. For now, a discussion of these added closing requirements will be shifted to later sections of this chapter, and this section will concentrate on how to close the books for a single-location private company.

As noted in Exhibit 2.1, the closing process follows multiple parallel paths, one for each of the functional accounting areas: payroll, invoicing, payables, inventory, and cash. These separate process flows also interact with each other; for example, nearly all accounts payable steps must be completed before one can roll new purchasing information into the fixed asset ledger or the overhead cost pools for subsequent allocation. Because of these interdependencies, some processing steps can be significantly delayed.

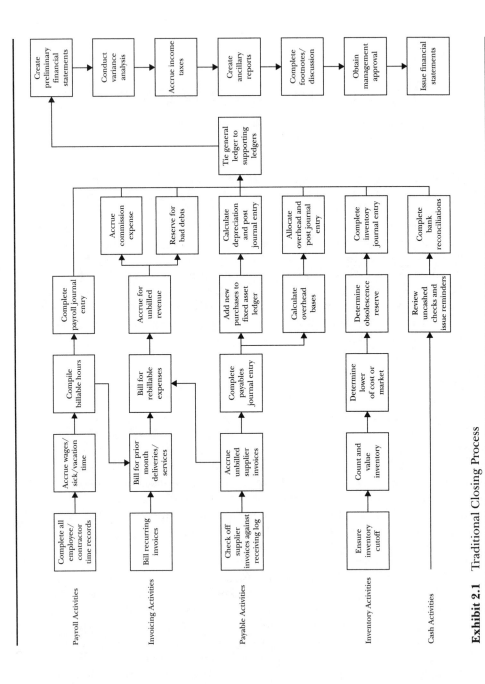

Exhibit 2.1 Traditional Closing Process

Controllers frequently wait while additional information arrives from outside sources before they are willing to complete a processing step. For example, they want to have a bank statement in hand before conducting a bank reconciliation; also, they may not close the accounts payable function until all significant supplier invoices have arrived.

The following points contain descriptions of the most common closing steps for each of the functional accounting areas:

- *Payroll activities.* If a company's payroll system does not produce paychecks on the last day of the month and include in those payments all time worked by employees through month-end, then some labor expenses are not being included in the financial statements. If so, the accounting staff typically spends a few days collecting time cards or similar documents from employees and calculating an accrued wage expense. They also must calculate the amount of accrued sick and vacation time and deduct from that figure any such time used by employees to see if accrual changes are required. Furthermore, they must extract from the payroll records the amount of any billable hours and forward this information to the invoicing staff for billing to customers. Finally, they use the payroll register from any payrolls run during the month to create one or more payroll journal entries to transfer payroll information to the general ledger; this last step may be automatic if the company runs its payroll in-house, or is compiled from paper documents if the company uses an outside payroll processing provider. Of all these activities, controllers sometimes ignore the wage and sick/vacation expense accruals, which can render the financial statements significantly inaccurate if wages are a large proportion of total company expenses.

- *Invoicing activities.* If a company issues recurring invoices for such items as periodic maintenance contracts, it typically issues them at the beginning of the month. A services company will also use billable hours information from the payroll staff and rebillable expense information from the payables staff to create invoices for services rendered. A product company will use shipping information from the warehouse (usually transmitted on paper) to create invoices for recent shipments. If shipment information has a history of being inaccurate, an accounting or internal auditing person may also be sent to the shipping dock to manually review the shipping log to ensure that all shipped items have been billed. Also, if services hours are earned but not billed, the accounting staff creates an accrued revenue journal entry. The controller also consults with the collections manager to update the reserve for bad debts, while accounting clerks create a spreadsheet listing commissions earned by each salesperson; the sales manager usually reviews this commission report and modifies it based on changes in commission splits, invoice allocations, and other criteria. The accounting staff modifies the commission report based on these changes and books a commission journal entry. Of all these activities, controllers tend to ignore regular updates to the reserve for bad debts, which places the company in the dangerous position of running out of reserves in a subsequent month and having to record an unusually large bad debt expense to rebuild its reserve.

- *Payable activities.* Although payables is not a difficult area to complete, controllers have a tendency to delay the closing in order to receive every last supplier invoice related to the period being closed. The more careful ones do this by obtaining a copy of the receiving log from the warehouse and checking off all invoices against it, waiting until every received item has a matching invoice. Once completed and rolled into the general ledger, this information is used to populate the fixed asset ledger and calculate depreciation, which in turn is also posted to the general ledger. Also, the completed payables information is rolled into cost pools for allocation to inventory. Thus, the accounts payable area is a significant bottleneck for key downstream closing activities.

- *Inventory activities.* Inventory is the area that gives controllers the most heartburn, because there is a risk of considerable inaccuracy in the reported figures. To prevent this problem, they tend to take extra time to ensure that the month-end cutoff has been properly completed and the inventory physically counted and valued. These steps can take many days, and so (like accounts payable) can be a bottleneck in the closing process. Additional closing steps are writing off inventory based on the lower of cost or market rule, as well as adjusting the reserve for obsolete inventory. These last two steps are frequently skipped by controllers, which is dangerous, because recording large expenses for these items only at year-end can be quite a shock to senior management and has led to the firing of more than a few controllers.

- *Cash activities.* Conducting a bank reconciliation seems like an easy closing activity, but it tends to be considerably delayed because some controllers insist on waiting until a physical bank statement arrives in the mail. Others delay the reconciliation until some time after the close has been completed, which underreports the amount of bank service fees listed on the bank statement. An added step regularly followed by more conscientious controllers is to regularly review uncashed checks and contact the payees to remind them to submit the checks to a bank for payment.

- *Additional activities.* The primary closing activities were noted earlier in Exhibit 2.1. However, other steps are necessary that will be specific to the circumstances of individual companies. For example, if there is outstanding debt at month-end, someone must calculate the amount of *accrued interest expense*. Also, if a company has entered into a royalty arrangement in exchange for its use of product designs, patented processes, and so on, then the *royalty expense* must also be accrued. Furthermore, there may be changes to the *equity accounts* caused by stock issuances, buybacks, or a company's recording of changes in its ownership interest in other entities, all of which require additional journal entries. Finally, a closing activity applicable to multiple functional areas is the detailed *account reconciliation*; this involves determining the exact contents of key accounts, such as accounts receivable and payable, prepaid expenses, and a variety of liability accounts. Listings of the contents of some accounts are commonly kept on electronic spreadsheets.

Thus, it is evident that many tasks must be completed in order to produce financial statements even for a relatively simple corporate configuration—one location with no public reporting. The situation can be made more difficult by introducing in the next section the additional tasks required to complete a close for a multidivision company.

ADDITIONAL CLOSING TASKS FOR THE MULTIDIVISION COMPANY

The corporate controller of a multidivision company will review the previous section and then loudly opine that the real bottleneck operation is missing— the forwarding of completed financial information from each division, which can take many days. The problem is exacerbated if the division controllers have no sense of urgency regarding the close and prefer to issue thoroughly reviewed and approved financial packages to the corporate accounting staff, sometimes many weeks after the reporting period. The problem is even worse if there are multiple levels of corporate reporting, so one company reports its results to its reporting parent, which reports to its parent, and so on. This arrangement can cause massive delays in the reporting process.

An additional issue for the multidivision company is mapping the charts of accounts (COAs) of all the reporting divisions to the corporate COA. If done manually, there is a considerable risk of mapping inconsistency from month to month, which can play havoc with subsequent variance analysis tasks. This is a particular problem for companies owning disparate business entities whose operational requirements really do require variations from the corporate COA.

Another issue is the identification and elimination of intercompany transactions. This is a significant task for companies whose business operations are heavily integrated both upstream and downstream. For example, a tire manufacturer that owns the raw rubber source, as well as retail tire outlets, must eliminate from its reported financial results any transactions between the various operating divisions prior to the final sale to customers.

This is a particular problem when the various divisions have freestanding accounting systems, because there is no automated approach for linking a sale on the books of one division to a receipt on the books of the division to whom the sale was made.

A final problem is analyzing and correcting the information supplied by the divisions. Because there are likely to be differences in the quality of information provided by each division, there is a reasonable chance that corporate-level variance analysis will uncover problems in the underlying transactions. Because the corporate accounting staff rarely has access to each division's individual transactions, it must forward investigation requests to the divisions and wait for them to conduct a review, which adds time to the closing process. Also, if a correcting entry is required, the corporate staff usually makes the change in the corporate books, which means that the corporate records of the division's results now vary from the division's in-house accounting records, requiring a periodic reconciliation to bring the two sets of books into alignment.

Thus, waiting for the financial results of subsidiaries, consolidating the information, eliminating intercompany transactions, and investigating and correcting problems in the consolidated results can add multiple weeks to the closing process—possibly several times more than are required for a single-location entity to report its financial results.

ADDITIONAL CLOSING TASKS FOR THE
MULTINATIONAL COMPANY

A multinational company (MNC) is, by definition, a multidivision company, so all of the additional closing tasks noted in the previous section also apply to the MNC. In addition, the MNC must convert the currencies in which the financial results of its divisions are reported into the reporting currency of the corporate office. Depending on a variety of criteria, the corporate accounting staff may use one of two translation methods (the current rate method or remeasurement method)[1] to make this conversion, and quite possibly use a different one for each division. The current rate method requires the retention of period-end exchange rate information for conversion purposes, whereas the remeasurement method requires the retention of additional exchange rates from earlier periods.

ADDITIONAL CLOSING TASKS FOR THE
PUBLIC CORPORATION

The publicly held company has considerable additional reporting tasks beyond those of a private firm. The SEC requires a specific reporting format (as detailed in its Regulation S-X) for financial statements. In addition, the annual 10-K and quarterly 10-Q reports require considerable additional disclosures. These reports are subject to intense SEC and investor scrutiny, so companies tend to spend lengthy periods reviewing their contents prior to issuance. If the underlying financial statements have been completed relatively quickly, the importance of issuing accurate 10-K or 10-Q reports leads many companies to still issue these documents only at the last minute, thereby giving them more time for document review.

The SEC requires public companies to file their annual 10-K reports within 60 days of year-end and their quarterly reports within 35 days of quarter-end, although slower reporting requirements are still acceptable for companies having a public float of less than $75 million (their reporting requirements are 90 and 45 days, respectively).

Exhibit 2.1 showed the basic closing tasks for a single-location company. Having just covered the additional reporting intricacies of multidivision, multinational, and public companies, the additional closing steps required by these entities are noted in the flowchart in Exhibit 2.2. A more comprehensive treatment of public company reporting requirements is located in Chapter 14.

PROBLEMS WITH THE CLOSING PROCESS

This section addresses some of the more common problems associated with the closing process. Solutions to these problems are discussed in subsequent chapters.

- *Management perfectionism.* There is an old wine advertisement starring Orson Welles, in which he said, "We will release no wine before its time." Some controllers are still not releasing financials before their time, which they seem to define as waiting for every conceivable supplier invoice to arrive and be logged in. This can make for a mighty long wait to see financial results, because some supplier invoices arrive long after month-end. Waiting for supplier invoices is not the only area in which key information arrives late—there can also be inventory recounts, bank statements, and expense rebillings to customers. Whatever the type of missing source document, there is a mindset problem where controllers want to be ultra-certain that the information they release is accurate. What these people do not understand is that financial statements are really a best guess at a company's financial position at any given point in time—that is why there are reserves for bad debts, inventory obsolescence, warranty claims, and so on that may not be proved accurate (or inaccurate) for many months to come.

- *Lack of procedures.* Go back to Exhibit 2.1 and count the number of closing steps. There are 31, and the exhibit shows only the most basic

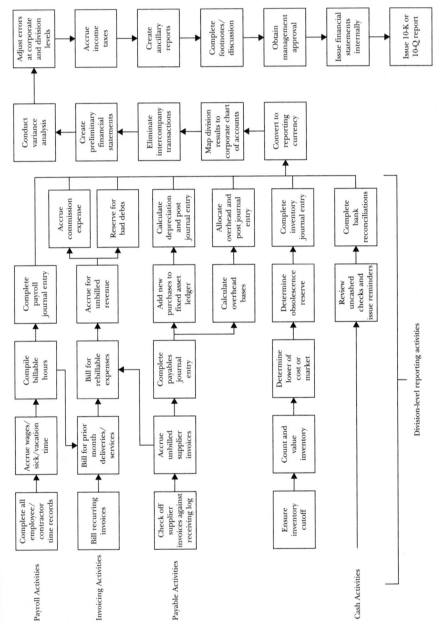

Exhibit 2.2 Closing Tasks for the Complex Enterprise

closing steps! The more complex Exhibit 2.2 shows 36 closing steps, and even that can be expanded substantially by a large corporation. Now, imagine dropping this complex closing process into a minimal level of organization. No one knows what steps to complete first, how steps are to be performed, or to whom they must then be sent. Not only is disorganization rampant, but the financial results also tend to be inconsistent from period to period, because different approaches may have been used each month to calculate such items as overhead allocations, bad debt reserves, or inventory obsolescence reserves. Furthermore, some steps may not have been completed at all, requiring surprise entries every few months to adjust for the missing entries. In short, combining a massive number of closing steps with a lack of organization yields a lengthy close and inaccurate financial statements.

- *Use of multiple accounting software packages.* If a company has several subsidiaries, it is a good bet that many of them use accounting software packages that differ not only from the corporate system but also from other divisions. Although each of these packages may operate quite well, it is likely that each one requires different procedures to operate and close at month-end. Thus, even if a company is slavishly devoted to the concept of enforcing procedures throughout the accounting department, the presence of different software at each location will probably result in multiple versions of the same procedures, one for each system in use. Maintaining up-to-date versions of these multiple procedure versions is difficult and time consuming. Also, if the corporate accounting staff needs information about the detailed contents of a specific account at the division level, it typically must contact the division accounting staff and ask for the information, rather than accessing it through a computer; this delay adds substantially to the variance analysis portion of the consolidation process.

- *Excessive decentralization.* The organization of the closing process in a multidivision company can cause a significant risk of fraud. The problem arises when the managers of individual reporting entities are given management control over the accounting departments of their operating units. By doing so, they can influence the reporting of financial information to corporate headquarters, not only through outright fraudulent transactions but also by influencing the calculation of measurements used to report operational results.

   Another problem with decentralization is that accounting departments at the division level must compile their accounting results and review and obtain local approval of the information before forwarding it to the corporate accounting staff for consolidation. This can result in an extremely long interval before the information ever arrives at corporate headquarters. It is a particular problem if there are multiple reporting levels, so that each successively higher level of accounting staff must wait for results from the lower-level entities before they can prepare their reports and forward them to the next-higher level of reporting entity.

- *Low-quality data.* The corporate accounting staff may do a sterling job of organizing accounting information into informative and GAAP-compliant financial statements and still issue extremely inaccurate information. The problem is caused by incorrect transactional data at the point of data entry. This is caused by several problems, including poor user training, inadequate automated data checking by the accounting software, and a lack of procedures for basic transactions. The cost to fix these problems at the corporate level is high and adds substantially to the time required to complete the closing process.

- *Varying charts of accounts.* One of the most common closing problems with multidivision companies is mapping the disparate divisional charts of accounts into a central chart of accounts. This process is highly error-prone and also subject to considerable interpretation, because the definition of an account may vary considerably between the division and corporate headquarters. The result is not only mapping errors but also inconsistency in the contents of accounts from period to period, resulting in wildly variable trend analyses for various accounts.

- *Use of electronic spreadsheets.* The typical accountant loves the electronic spreadsheet; it is so simple to extract data from a general ledger, manipulate information in the spreadsheet, and use the results to enter adjusting journal entries back into the general ledger. However, this process requires manual intervention and is subject to errors caused by both data entry mistakes and incorrect spreadsheet formulas. Another problem arises when the creator of an especially complex spreadsheet leaves the company, leaving no one who understands how it works. Some multilocation companies use electronic spreadsheets so extensively that there is no corporate accounting software at all— they just consolidate divisional financial results into a spreadsheet and use that as the foundation for all financial reports. Thus, excessive electronic spreadsheet use results in possible reporting errors, the introduction of manual labor into the closing process, and excessive reliance on specialized staff knowledgeable in spreadsheet use.

- *Multiple report formats.* Once the corporate accounting staff has completed its consolidation of financial information, it may still require many days before it can issue financial statements, because company management requires so many versions of the same reports. Some reports are issued at the division level, others to senior corporate managers, others to the investing public, others to creditors and lenders, and so on. Creating so many variations on the same reporting package can introduce multiple days of effort to the closing process.

- *Linkage to fraud.* The longer the closing process, the greater the opportunity for fraud to be introduced into the closing process. For example, if a close is regularly completed in one day, there is no way for anyone to record late deliveries as revenue in the prior month, because the financials have already been published. Conversely, a lengthy closing period allows management to spend days pondering ways to favorably alter the reported financial results. Also, if the accounting staff at the corporate level is intent on presenting an excessively rosy picture of the company's results, it can alter the financial information forwarded to it by the various company divisions, without the divisions even being aware of any changes being made.

- *Involvement of third parties.* If a company is publicly held, it must work with several third parties to issue its 10-Q and 10-K reports to the SEC. This includes outside auditors, attorneys, the corporate audit committee, and a firm that reformats and files the reports with the SEC. These entities all have their own resource constraints and resulting work schedules that may severely lengthen the duration of the filing process.

SUMMARY

The main point to take away from this chapter is that the closing process initially appears to be a frighteningly complex and tangled mess through which the controller must painfully navigate—every month. However, as discussed in subsequent chapters, there are a multitude of ways to more efficiently manage the closing process, resulting in a much faster close than would at first appear possible. In the next chapter, a simple process analysis is followed to extract some key information from the reporting process, which allows achievement of a fast close in subsequent chapters.

ENDNOTE

1. For more information about currency conversion methods, see Chapter 16 of Bragg, *GAAP* Policies adn Procedures Manual, 5th Edition (Hoboken, NJ: John Wiley & Sons, Inc., 2007).

3

Conducting a Review of the Closing Process

Chapter 2 pointed out the large number of steps required to complete a quality month-end closing, and then went on to describe some inherent problems with the closing process. Before attempting to fix these problems, it is useful to first break down each of the process flows associated with the closing to determine the sources and uses of information, wait and process times, responsibilities by task, and error rates. By doing so, it becomes much easier to dissect every element of the closing to determine where improvements should be made and in what order. The remainder of this chapter does so for every major process within the financial close.

STEPS IN THE PROCESS REVIEW

Documenting the closing process is not as simple as just listing the sequence of events in the process. A great deal of additional information is required to learn about all aspects of the close. A better approach is to divide the close into the major process flows, which are payroll, payables, billings, inventory, and cash. An additional set of processes addresses final closing tasks, including conversion to the reporting currency, eliminating inter-company transactions, conducting final variance analysis, and so on.

An example of a detailed process analysis is shown in Exhibit 3.1, which shows a great deal of information about payroll closing tasks. The exhibit shows a flowchart[1] in the first three columns, accompanied by explanatory information in the next four columns, which are described as follows:

- *Inputs.* The analysis begins with inputs to the process, which in this case is time cards. A knowledge of source data can be useful if altering the core process will be impacted by the timing of incoming data. This information flows through the basic closing process, which is listed in the second column.

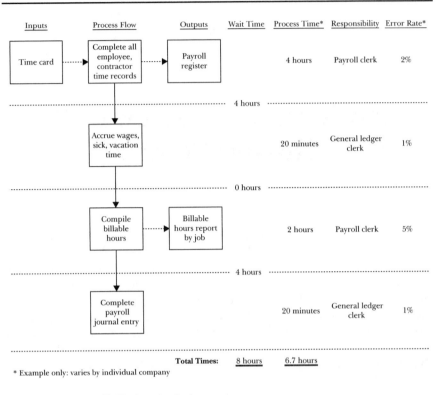

Inputs	Process Flow	Outputs	Wait Time	Process Time*	Responsibility	Error Rate*
Time card	Complete all employee, contractor time records	Payroll register		4 hours	Payroll clerk	2%
			4 hours			
	Accrue wages, sick, vacation time			20 minutes	General ledger clerk	1%
			0 hours			
	Compile billable hours	Billable hours report by job		2 hours	Payroll clerk	5%
			4 hours			
	Complete payroll journal entry			20 minutes	General ledger clerk	1%
		Total Times:	8 hours	6.7 hours		

* Example only: varies by individual company

Exhibit 3.1   Payroll Closing Analysis

- *Process flow.* The second column shows the sequential flow of processes required to close the accounting records. Although this can be a complex flowcharting analysis, consider combining or eliminating minor processing steps in order to give the reader a quicker grasp of the general flow of information.

- *Outputs.* A few outputs from the process appear in the third column; these reports may be more extensive than anyone suspects, because reports were requested for short-term needs and never canceled once the needs were fulfilled. Also, the information on several reports may be merged onto fewer reports.

- *Wait time.* The wait times shown in the fourth column are among the most critical ones from the perspective of eliminating excess time from the closing process. They are usually longer than the actual processing time and frequently occur because a processing step has shifted from the initiating person to another person—in many cases, this is queue time.

- *Process time*. The fifth column shows the time actually required to complete each step in the process flow. Although this area certainly requires attention, it tends to be smaller than the wait times in the preceding column; it is of considerable importance when targeting which processes to improve first, because putting a massive time and investment effort into the improvement of a small processing interval is clearly not a good use of company resources.

- *Responsibility*. The sixth column lists the job position responsible for each process step. This is closely associated with wait times, because shifting tasks from one person to another will necessarily require the inclusion of each step in successive employee work queues.

- *Error rate*. The seventh and final column notes the error rate associated with each process step. This is important information, because the time required to locate and correct an error can greatly exceed the time that would otherwise be needed to complete the entire processing step. It is best to keep error information as current as possible, so only list error percentages reflecting actual error rates for the past quarter on a rolling basis.

In Exhibit 3.1, note that the information listed in several columns will not be the same as is found in company-specific circumstances. Processing times will vary considerably, depending on internal procedures, transaction volumes, error rates, and transaction efficiency. Similarly, error rates will vary depending on staff training, internal procedures, and the existing framework of controls.

Another point about the information presented in Exhibit 3.1 is that this is not an overly detailed document—there has been no attempt to itemize every conceivable processing step, control points, intermediate reports issued for review purposes, the types of transactional errors, and so on. Instead, the presented process review document strikes a balance between comprehensive knowledge of the process and having a good overview of how it works. In this way, controllers can quickly move from analyzing the closing process to taking swift action steps to shorten the process. However, when consolidating processing steps for this analysis, be sure to separate and clearly identify those steps requiring a great deal of processing or wait times, as well as those resulting in a significant proportion of transactional errors, because these areas must be targeted for process improvement.

A final point about process analysis is that the first draft is almost certainly going to contain some incorrect information, given the difficulties of data collection. Consequently, be sure to verify the information with the accounting staff and anyone outside of the department who contributes information to the closing process, and then revise the document accordingly.

It is useful to also analyze Exhibit 3.1, not only as a general example of a process review document, but also as an analysis of the payroll process in particular. There are three points of interest in the analysis. First, the key bottleneck is the receipt of time card information, because that not only can take a great deal of time, but it is also required for all subsequent processing steps. The second point is the potentially long wait time required before the general ledger clerk can make journal entries to record payroll transactions in the general ledger. Third, the error rates associated with both the initial recording of time card data and the compilation of billable hours can significantly delay the entire payroll closing process. These issues will be dealt with in Chapter 10.

PAYABLES PROCESS REVIEW

Exhibit 3.2 shows the process review for the accounts payable process. This tends to be a major bottleneck area for the closing process, and so is worthy of some review. The first point to consider is the inordinate number of hours of processing time shown in the analysis to accrue unbilled supplier invoices; although three business days is a general estimate, it is reasonable for most companies to wait about this long before they are reasonably certain to have received most supplier invoices and can accrue for the remainder. Another problem is the delay required before the fixed assets ledger and associated depreciation expenses can be calculated, because it is customary to close accounts payable prior to beginning work on the fixed assets ledger. Also, note in the bottom right-hand corner of the exhibit the high error rates associated with calculating overhead bases and allocating overhead costs; this is caused by the commonly used manual extraction of data from the general ledger into an electronic spreadsheet for data manipulation and then back into the general ledger. By introducing spreadsheets into the closing process, there are not only more chances for data entry errors to occur but also for the misinterpretation or incorrect calculation of the resulting information. These issues will be dealt with in Chapter 11.

BILLING PROCESS REVIEW

The billing process depends on the completion of other processes, requires the involvement of multiple staff positions, and can also result in high transaction error rates, all of which contribute to a potentially major blockage in a company's ability to conclude even a reasonably fast close.

Exhibit 3.3 shows the closing difficulties inherent in the billing process. First, the billings clerk typically must complete recurring invoices before even addressing any additional invoices based on month-end shipments or labor hours worked. Second, those additional invoices cannot be created until either the shipping department (for goods delivered) or payroll department (for services delivered) has completed its input documents for the

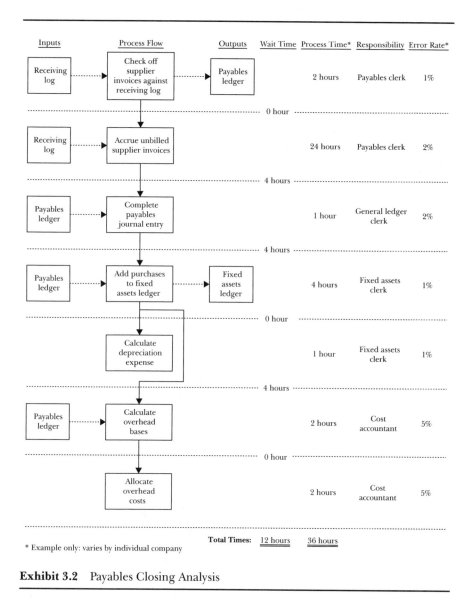

Inputs	Process Flow	Outputs	Wait Time	Process Time*	Responsibility	Error Rate*
Receiving log	Check off supplier invoices against receiving log	Payables ledger		2 hours	Payables clerk	1%
			0 hour			
Receiving log	Accrue unbilled supplier invoices			24 hours	Payables clerk	2%
			4 hours			
Payables ledger	Complete payables journal entry			1 hour	General ledger clerk	2%
			4 hours			
Payables ledger	Add purchases to fixed assets ledger	Fixed assets ledger		4 hours	Fixed assets clerk	1%
			0 hour			
	Calculate depreciation expense			1 hour	Fixed assets clerk	1%
			4 hours			
Payables ledger	Calculate overhead bases			2 hours	Cost accountant	5%
			0 hour			
	Allocate overhead costs			2 hours	Cost accountant	5%

Total Times: 12 hours   36 hours

* Example only: varies by individual company

Exhibit 3.2   Payables Closing Analysis

billing process and forwarded them to the billings clerk. A major delay can arise if expenses are being rebilled to customers, because the billings clerk must wait to create invoices until the payables staff has closed the payables ledger and charged expenses to specific billable jobs, which can require multiple days if the payables department manager prefers to wait for all possible supplier invoices from the preceding month to arrive in the mail. Furthermore, some expenses can be rebilled to customers while others

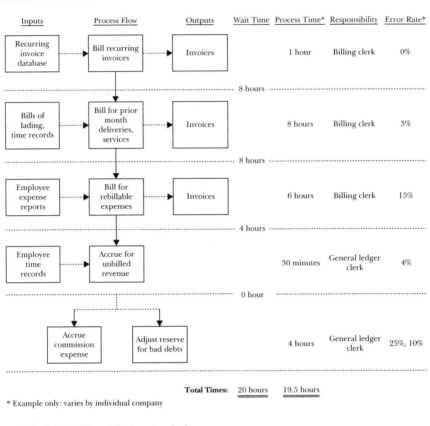

Inputs	Process Flow	Outputs	Wait Time	Process Time*	Responsibility	Error Rate*
Recurring invoice database	Bill recurring invoices	Invoices		1 hour	Billing clerk	0%
			8 hours			
Bills of lading, time records	Bill for prior month deliveries, services	Invoices		8 hours	Billing clerk	3%
			8 hours			
Employee expense reports	Bill for rebillable expenses	Invoices		6 hours	Billing clerk	15%
			4 hours			
Employee time records	Accrue for unbilled revenue			30 minutes	General ledger clerk	4%
			0 hour			
	Accrue commission expense	Adjust reserve for bad debts		4 hours	General ledger clerk	25%, 10%

Total Times: 20 hours   19.5 hours

* Example only: varies by individual company

Exhibit 3.3   Billing Closing Analysis

must be charged to expense; depending on the level of internal documentation, it may not be immediately clear how to treat expenses, which calls for lengthy internal reviews before related invoices can finally be sent to customers—all of which requires extra time within the closing process.

Another problem is the calculation of commissions, which must be accrued as part of the closing process. Some commission plans are so convoluted that it is impossible to automate commission calculations, whereas manual calculations are subject to a high degree of error that requires multiple iterations before an accurate commission expense can be accrued. These issues will be dealt with in Chapter 9.

INVENTORY PROCESS REVIEW

A great many controllers consider the inventory component of the close to be the riskiest area, given the high probability of recording an incorrect

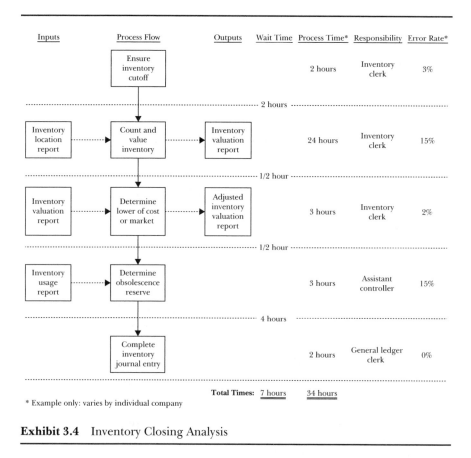

Inputs	Process Flow	Outputs	Wait Time	Process Time*	Responsibility	Error Rate*
	Ensure inventory cutoff			2 hours	Inventory clerk	3%
			·········· 2 hours ··········			
Inventory location report	Count and value inventory	Inventory valuation report		24 hours	Inventory clerk	15%
			·········· 1/2 hour ··········			
Inventory valuation report	Determine lower of cost or market	Adjusted inventory valuation report		3 hours	Inventory clerk	2%
			·········· 1/2 hour ··········			
Inventory usage report	Determine obsolescence reserve			3 hours	Assistant controller	15%
			·········· 4 hours ··········			
	Complete inventory journal entry			2 hours	General ledger clerk	0%
		Total Times:	7 hours	34 hours		

* Example only: varies by individual company

Exhibit 3.4   Inventory Closing Analysis

inventory valuation, and so tend to spend a large proportion of the closing effort on this area. The closing analysis in Exhibit 3.4 clarifies this issue by showing a large amount of time devoted to the counting and valuation of inventory (three business days, which can vary considerably by company). It is not uncommon to count the inventory several times before a controller is comfortable with the resulting cost of goods sold.

The exhibit includes several steps that controllers tend to ignore, which are the determination of lower of cost or market, as well as the correct size of the inventory obsolescence reserve. The inventory obsolescence area receives either minimal attention on a monthly basis (resulting in large adjustments at year-end) or continual reviews as part of every monthly closing (usually by controllers who have previously been burned by large write-offs in this area). In any event, the obsolescence review tends to be disorganized, so the resulting reserve can be inaccurate (hence the large error rate listed in the exhibit). These issues will be dealt with in Chapter 8.

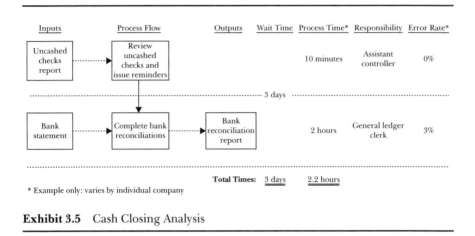

Exhibit 3.5   Cash Closing Analysis

CASH PROCESS REVIEW

There is only one major delay associated with the cash closing process, but it can require a wait of three or four business days—the arrival of the month-end bank statement. This is the source document needed to complete the bank reconciliation. If there are several bank accounts and therefore multiple statements arriving on the same day, this causes a bottleneck on the part of whomever is in charge of bank reconciliations. The process analysis is shown in Exhibit 3.5.

There are several ways not only to reduce the time required for the bank reconciliation but also to remove it from the month-end closing process. These issues will be dealt with in Chapter 12.

FINAL CLOSING PROCESS REVIEW

Once all of the traditional functional areas have completed their month-end closing processes, there are still a series of additional steps to complete before financial statements can be issued to the general public. These steps, with associated closing information, are shown in Exhibit 3.6.

The exhibit reveals four areas of interest. First, mapping divisional reporting to the corporate COA is a manual and highly error-prone process that can require multiple iterations of the financial statements before all information has been mapped correctly. Second, intercompany transactions are difficult to find, so their elimination tends to be a haphazard affair that frequently results in excessively high reported revenue levels. Third, any errors found during corporate-level analysis of the financial statements must be adjusted on both the corporate and division books, which raises the possibility of not recording the same entry on both sets

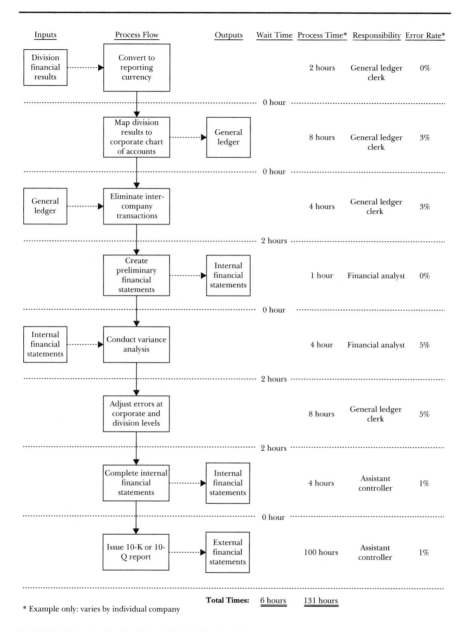

Inputs	Process Flow	Outputs	Wait Time	Process Time*	Responsibility	Error Rate*
Division financial results	Convert to reporting currency			2 hours	General ledger clerk	0%
			0 hour			
	Map division results to corporate chart of accounts	General ledger		8 hours	General ledger clerk	3%
			0 hour			
General ledger	Eliminate inter-company transactions			4 hours	General ledger clerk	3%
			2 hours			
	Create preliminary financial statements	Internal financial statements		1 hour	Financial analyst	0%
			0 hour			
Internal financial statements	Conduct variance analysis			4 hour	Financial analyst	5%
			2 hours			
	Adjust errors at corporate and division levels			8 hours	General ledger clerk	5%
			2 hours			
	Complete internal financial statements	Internal financial statements		4 hours	Assistant controller	1%
			0 hour			
	Issue 10-K or 10-Q report	External financial statements		100 hours	Assistant controller	1%
	Total Times:		6 hours	131 hours		

* Example only: varies by individual company

Exhibit 3.6   Analysis of the Final Closing Process

of books. Finally, controllers tend to take an extremely long time to issue public financial statements (10-Q or 10-K reports), because they want to review financial information until the due date required by law. Thus, even if the financial statements are completed in short order, multiple weeks

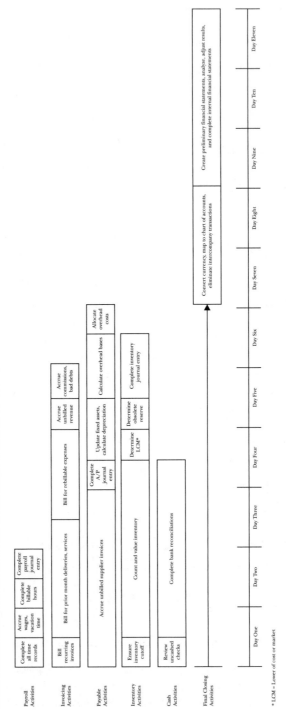

Payroll Activities	Complete all time records	Accrue wages, vacation time	Complete billable hours	Complete payroll journal entry						
Invoicing Activities	Bill recurring invoices	Bill for prior month deliveries, services		Bill for rebillable expenses	Accrue unbilled revenue	Accrue commissions, bad debts				
Payable Activities		Accrue unbilled supplier invoices		Complete A/P journal entry	Update fixed assets, calculate depreciation	Calculate overhead bases	Allocate overhead costs			
Inventory Activities	Ensure inventory cutoff	Count and value inventory		Determine LCM*	Determine obsolete reserve	Complete inventory journal entry				
Cash Activities	Review uncashed checks	Complete bank reconciliations								
Final Closing Activities							Convert currency, map to chart of accounts, eliminate intercompany transactions	Create preliminary financial statements, analyze, adjust results, and complete internal financial statements		
	Day One	Day Two	Day Three	Day Four	Day Five	Day Six	Day Seven	Day Eight	Day Nine	Day Ten	Day Eleven

* LCM = Lower of cost or market

Exhibit 3.7 Combined Closing Timeline

(or months) can pass before the final statements are issued to the public. These issues and others will be dealt with in Chapters 7 and 14.

TOTAL DURATION OF THE CLOSING PROCESS

Although the closing process has been broken down into a fair degree of detail to see how each function is involved in the close, it is not yet clear how all activities work together to create the combined close. This information is shown in Exhibit 3.7.

The timeline shows closing activities within four-hour time blocks, with preceding wait times included in the processing time for each activity. As noted earlier, the time periods shown here are only estimates and will vary by company. Also, the timeline assumes a multilocation company that must spend extra time consolidating divisional results; single-location companies will require substantially less time to complete the final closing activities. However, the timeline does *not* include the extra time required to create reports for the general public, because the completion of 10-Q or 10-K reports would extend the timeline a long way to the right.

Exhibit 3.7 reveals that a company can take 11 business days to complete financial statements, although the closing of all underlying processes requires only about one-half of the total interval. Also, there are several activities in which substantial wait times are incorporated, such as the accrual of unbilled supplier invoices, completing bank reconciliations, and billing for rebillable expenses. The compression of these wait times will be a key topic in subsequent chapters.

SUMMARY

Through the use of closing analyses for each of the major functional areas within the closing process, this chapter has provided several clues for how to create a fast close. Also, the time required to close the books using a traditional closing process was itemized. The rest of this book addresses a wide range of techniques for how to use this information to create a fast close. In the next chapter, the timing of selected closing steps is altered, which is an easy and cost-effective way to quickly reduce the time needed to close the books.

ENDNOTE

1. For more information about flowcharting, refer to Chapter 3 of Bragg, *Policies and Procedures Manual*, 5th Edition, (Hoboken, NJ: John Wiley & Sons, Inc., 2007).

4

Alter the Timing of Closing Activities

Consulting firms advertise that they can assist a company in achieving a fast close, usually through the installation of an expensive ERP system that costs millions of dollars. Although such installations can shrink the closing interval, they also require the wealth of a maharajah or small oil nation to implement. An infinitely better approach is to first run through a series of simple, virtually free changes in the closing activities to achieve quick and substantial improvements. The most effective of all these free changes is presented in this chapter—altering the timing of closing activities.

ALTERING THE CLOSING MINDSET

The typical controller thinks that the closing process starts on the first day of the new month with a sudden rush of several dozen activities to be completed, all within a frightfully small time interval. However, a surprising number of activities can be either partially or completely shifted out of the core closing period, either by moving them into the last few days of the preceding month or by recognizing that they are not central to the closing mission and deferring them until later in the month. This is more than a scheduling change, involving an alteration in mindset, because changing activity timing can slightly alter the accuracy of the resulting information. The controller needs to realize that minor accuracy issues do not have a significant impact on reported financial results and can easily be corrected in the following month's financial statements. These accuracy issues will be noted throughout this chapter.

The following sections address how specific closing activities can be shifted out of the core closing period. They are generally described in the order in which they would be completed, with the early-completion items listed first. At the end of the chapter, how these scheduling changes impact the month-end activities checklist and compress the time required to produce financial statements is discussed.

REVIEW AND CORRECT SUBLEDGER TRANSACTIONS THROUGHOUT THE MONTH

The core closing period is a bad time to initially learn about transaction errors, especially if they are located in a subsidiary's accounting system to which the corporate analysis staff does not have direct access. Such problems call for a last-minute fire drill to determine the nature of the problem and correct it—both in the corporate and subsidiary accounting records. Also, given the extremely abbreviated time period in which these changes must be corrected, it is unlikely that the accounting staff can thoroughly analyze the reason for the mistake and ensure through systemic changes that it will not arise again.

An excellent alternative is to institute a continuous process of reviewing and correcting subledger transactions throughout the month. A common interval is to conduct this review weekly. By doing so, the number of trans-actional errors discovered during the closing process will likely plummet. In addition, and of more importance over the long term from the standpoint of accounting efficiency, these regular reviews allow the accounting staff sufficient time to improve processes and permanently reduce the overall number of transactional errors.

COMPLETE THE BANK RECONCILIATION EVERY DAY

Professors teach college accounting students to wait for the monthly bank statement and use it to conduct a bank reconciliation. Unfortunately, this training leaves many accountants unwilling to venture forth into an online banking experience, which allows for daily reconciliations. To do so, set up a bank account where the bank allows access to online balance information, as well as detailed check clearing, deposit, and bank fee information. Then print the daily results and enter them into the accounting software's bank reconciliation module. It may also be possible to set up two windows on the computer screen, so that one window shows the bank information and the other the reconciliation software; then visually transfer the information over to the reconciliation module.

This approach completely eliminates the need to wait days for the printed bank reconciliation to arrive. It is also an excellent control point, because no more than one day passes before any cash-related anomalies will become immediately apparent to the person conducting the reconciliation.

There are only a few minor problems with completing a daily recon-ciliation. First, there tend to be more journal entries, because you make entries every day, rather than waiting until month-end to add them all into a single large entry. Second, it takes somewhat more time to complete about 20 short daily reconciliations than a single large monthly one. Finally, there will be a delay in recording interest income and perhaps bank fees, because banks usually record that information in the bank account subsequent to month-end. If these items are minor, it is reasonable to record them in the following month, so there is a perpetual one-month lag in recognizing these expenses and income. Alternatively, if this is a substantial sum, create a journal entry for estimated interest income or bank fees, and then adjust it in the following month when the actual figure arrives on the bank statement.

REVIEW UNCASHED CHECKS

A picky controller may choose to review uncashed checks as part of the closing process and encourage recipients to cash them, thereby avoiding any problems with unclaimed property laws at the state level. However, there is no particular need to attach this step to the closing, as long as it is conducted at regularly scheduled intervals throughout the year. Consequently, add this step to the accounting department's activity calendar, but as far away from more critical closing activities as possible.

UPDATE THE INVENTORY OBSOLESCENCE RESERVE

A critical error for many controllers is to not update the inventory obsolescence reserve on a regularly scheduled basis, because unrecognized losses in this area can pile up until there is a substantial write-off at the end of the reporting year. It is much more prudent to conduct an obsolescence review regularly in order to record significant changes in a timely manner. Some controllers take this concept to the opposite extreme by requiring an update as part of every closing process. This is not necessary, as long as the review is completed at regularly scheduled intervals. Thus, make sure that the accounting department will formally address the issue periodically, but schedule it away from more critical closing steps.

DETERMINE THE LOWER OF COST OR MARKET

As was the case with the inventory obsolescence reserve, many controllers do not regularly review the lower of cost or market (LCM) valuation of inventory, which can result in large write-offs at year-end. To avoid this, schedule regular LCM reviews, although not necessarily coincident with the month-end closing.

CALCULATE OVERHEAD ALLOCATION BASES

The traditional approach to allocating overhead expenses is to compile the operating measurement on which overhead costs are allocated, such as direct labor hours, from the preceding month and then use it to allocate the contents of the overhead pools to inventory or the cost of goods sold. There are two problems with this approach. First, the measurement information being collected is usually nonfinancial in nature, and so the data collection system may not be as efficient as a system based on financial transactions. Second, the allocation information cannot be collected until the month has closed, which can prolong the closing process.

To circumvent these problems, consider using an allocation based on operating results with a lag of one month, a rolling average of several previous months, or some similar concept. Unless production activity levels vary drastically from month to month, this will probably result in a reasonably accurate allocation system. Another alternative is to allocate based on budgeted activity levels, although this approach can be inaccurate if actual activity levels have diverged substantially from budgeted expectations. However, if a rolling budget is used, budgeted activity levels are much more likely to align with actual activity, making this a more palatable option.

BILL RECURRING INVOICES

Issuing recurring invoices tends to be parked on the list of closing activities on closing day, even though there is no reason to do so as part of the close. In fact, there is no reason to do it even the day before the close, because the precise amount of recurring invoices is typically known far in advance of the closing date. Instead, print these invoices a week before month-end, setting the date of the accounting software forward to reflect the date on which they are supposed to be printed; this records the associated revenue in the proper month, rather than in the preceding month.

This approach also accelerates collection, because by immediately putting recurring invoices in the mail as soon as they are printed, they are certain to be sitting on recipients' desks as of the first day of the month for approval, rather than several days later. Furthermore, the information on the recurring invoices tends to be more accurate, because the billings clerk is under absolutely no pressure to issue the invoices as part of the closing process, and so can conduct a leisurely review to ensure that each invoice contains the correct information.

A variation on the recurring invoice is the one-time fixed-fee invoice. Even if the job related to such an invoice is not yet finished prior to month-end, if there is a high expectation of it being done by closing day, go ahead and print the invoice (using as the invoice date the day of anticipated job completion). Then retain the invoice until closing day, verify that the job was actually completed on time, and mail it to the customer. If the job was not completed on time, delete the invoice from the system. Because invoice deletion typically takes less time to complete than originating the invoice, this still represents a time savings over waiting until closing day to create the invoice.

CONDUCT A PRELIMINARY COMPARISON OF THE SHIPPING LOG TO INVOICES ISSUED

A common practice for the more paranoid controller is to have someone manually compare the shipping log to invoices issued, to ensure that every delivery has a matching invoice. Although this approach can take a considerable amount of time during the closing, it also ensures maximum revenue and is especially worthwhile if there is a history of billing control problems.

If the controller feels that this step is needed, then consider splitting the reviewing task into two pieces—the first part to be conducted prior to month-end, and covering all monthly shipments up to that point, and the second part to remain in the core closing period, but only to include shipments for the last day or two of the month. This approach at least spreads out the task, even if it does not eliminate it.

REVIEW PRELIMINARY REBILLABLE EXPENSES

As noted later in this chapter, the act of issuing invoices for rebillable expenses should be deferred until after the closing process is completed. However, it is still necessary to conduct a preliminary review of these expenses prior to month-end for two reasons. First, it is possible that some expenses have crept into the rebillable expense accounts that are not really rebillable. If so, they must be charged to an expense account at once, which reduces the level of reported profitability. Second, it takes time to obtain expense reports from employees in the field, many of which can be rebilled, so it is useful to conduct an early scan of these expenses to determine which ones are missing and to remind employees to send in their expenses. Otherwise, the same reminding process must be done *after* the closing process, resulting in further delays in the delivery of invoices for rebillable expenses.

UPDATE THE BAD DEBT RESERVE

The bad debt reserve is essentially an estimate of the percentage of accounts receivable that the collections staff feels will never be collected. Because this is an estimate and therefore not an especially precise figure, there is no reason not to derive the estimate a day or two before month-end rather than afterward—this is hardly likely to alter the amount of bad debt accrual. The only issue is if the reserve is based on a fixed percentage of the total accounts receivable at month-end, which is a figure subject to last-minute billings. If so, estimate the amount of these last-minute billings in order to calculate the reserve. If the estimate is substantially incorrect (which it should not be if the company has any forecasting system at all for billings to be created one day in the future!), the reserve will still probably not be impacted much, because the reserve is typically a very small percentage of total billings.

REVIEW PRELIMINARY BILLABLE HOURS

If a company issues a large proportion of its month-end billings on the basis of staff hours worked, the accounting department may find itself inundated during the core closing period with the detailed analysis of hours worked by job prior to entering this information into invoices. A careful analysis of hours worked is usually necessary in order to avoid customer nonpayment of invoices for a variety of reasons: hours incorrectly coded to the wrong job, hours charged exceeding authorized limits, incorrect labor rates, and so on. In addition, a few employees usually have not entered hours into the time reporting system for the billing period and must be tracked down and reminded.

To avoid these problems, conduct the review just prior to month-end, scanning time records for the most common data entry errors and missing entries, as well as in comparison to remaining billable balances by job. There will still be a small amount of review work to be done during the core closing period, but it will be for only the last working day or so of the reporting period—all other time records will have been corrected by then.

ACCRUE INTEREST EXPENSE

If a company has outstanding debt, there should be a charge to interest expense that accurately reflects the amount outstanding throughout the month. Controllers typically wait until the month has closed before making this entry in order to incorporate into the expense calculation any last-minute changes in the debt balance. However, if a change occurs within just a day or two of month-end, how much will this really change the total interest expense? Unless the amount of debt is extremely large, completing the interest accrual a day or two before month-end will have little impact on the total interest expense charged. Also, it is sometimes possible to anticipate when the debt level is about to change, so one can make an accrual that anticipates these changes, thereby making the accrual even more accurate.

Even if there is some inaccuracy in the interest accrual, it is always possible to modify the following month's accrual in order to adjust for any last-minute debt changes that were not reflected in the last month's interest expense accrual.

DETERMINE PENSION PLAN FUNDING

If a company regularly funds a defined benefit or contribution pension plan, it can easily create the journal entry to reflect the funding of this plan as soon as the final payroll of the month has been run. All the information needed to determine funding is available at that point, so the funding entry can be comfortably placed several days prior to month-end. For example, if a company always pays its employees on the last business day of the month, the payroll is typically run about three days prior to that point, along with the payroll register that is commonly used as the foundation for a pension plan funding calculation. One then has sufficient time to create the funding calculation in a fairly leisurely manner.

If there is a significant time period between the last payroll register and month-end, then the amount of pension plan funding may be large enough to warrant the creation of an additional pension accrual, which can be roughly estimated based on the number of employee days worked through the accrual period. This additional entry can still be completed prior to month-end.

DETERMINE FLEXIBLE SPENDING ACCOUNT FUNDING

As was the case for pension plans, any deductions from employee pay-checks are typically recorded several days prior to month-end in the final payroll register. Because of the ready accessibility of this information, there is no reason why the information cannot be used to move funds prior to month-end from the corporate bank account to a flexible spending account for immediate use by employees. This entry has no impact on the income statement, but it does increase the amount of restricted cash, and so has a small impact on the accuracy of the balance sheet.

If there is a significant time period between the last payroll register and month-end, the amount of incremental flexible spending deductions to be withheld from employee pay for this extra time period is typically so small that there is no need to make an entry.

ACCRUE UNPAID WAGES

In some companies where many employees are paid on an hourly basis, the size of the month-end wage accrual can be substantial. In such companies, the accounting staff may consider the wage accrual to be the most important accrual they complete, and they will spend a considerable amount of time collecting handwritten time cards in order to calculate an accurate accrual.

In order to prevent this accrual from inordinately delaying the closing process, some controllers authorize a guesstimate of hours worked for the period between when the last time cards were submitted and the end of the month. If the workforce is stable and consistently works the same number of hours each day, this may be grounds for a reasonably accurate wage accrual that can be completed prior to month-end.

An alternative is to use a central timekeeping system to obtain the most current information about hours worked and generate the accrual from that central database at the end of the day just prior to the core closing period. If not all of the timekeeping information is available at this point, the missing hours may constitute such a small proportion of the accrual that the accounting staff can reasonably estimate the size of the wages associated with the unrecorded hours. Several types of timekeeping systems are available, such as an Internet-based system (accessible by employees anywhere there is Internet access) or intelligent time-tracking terminals that are tied to a central database (more useful for single locations where there are many hourly employees). No matter what system is used, some employee training (and reminding) will be required to ensure that everyone enters his or her time into the system as soon as possible.

ACCRUE UNUSED VACATION TIME

Many controllers do not review the vacation accrual frequently, preferring to issue a modifying accrual once a quarter or even as little as once a year. However, this approach may not yield accurate results if a company is growing or shrinking rapidly with attendant changes in headcount, and especially if there are high rates of pay combined with large vacation allowances. If so, the vacation accrual could have a significant impact on reported financial results.

If it is necessary to compile a vacation accrual every month, the best time to do so is immediately after the last payroll register of the month has been completed. This document contains records of the most recent vacation hours used by employees and may also include the number of vacation hours available to each employee (a common feature offered by application service providers). There are several ways to proceed with this information. One is to transfer the payroll information directly into a vacation accrual spreadsheet for eventual translation into an adjusting journal entry; however, this approach does not include any vacation hours earned or taken during the interval between the last payroll pay date and the end of the month. If the company has an online time-tracking system, a better option is to require employees to update their time information through a point as close to month-end as possible and use this additional information to fine-tune the vacation accrual.

ACCRUE TRAVEL EXPENSES

In most companies, the controller sees travel expenses only after someone returns from a trip and files an expense report. This can have a significant impact if employees are in the habit of filing expense reports late or of letting the expenses from multiple trips pile up before they submit a really large expense report. If profitability levels are low to begin with, the arrival of such expenses constitutes an extremely unwelcome surprise that can create a loss for the month.

Although rarely used, it is possible to accrue travel expenses before expense reports come anywhere near the accounting department. One approach is to require that all airfares be requested through a central travel agency; if the agency issues to the controller a month-end report detailing all travel during the month by employees, it is not difficult to create a reasonably accurate estimate of airfare and hotel costs (as supplied by the travel agency), as well as a per-diem meals cost based on the departure and return dates on air travel as reported by the travel agency. Another alternative that requires additional paperwork is to require centralized approval of all trips, so that trip information can be compiled by an internal source. Of the two options, requiring employees to use a central travel agency involves less bureaucracy and can result in somewhat more accurate expense information.

RECONCILE ASSET AND LIABILITY ACCOUNTS

A prudent controller will insist on having a complete list of detailed account analyses as part of the financial statements. Doing so will ensure that no unusual assets or liabilities are parked on the balance sheet when they should have been flushed out through the income statement. However, it also takes time to prepare this information, which can clog up the closing process.

The simplest approach is to prepare the detailed account analyses on the last day of the preceding month, when there is more time for a thoughtful review of these accounts. Although there is still a risk of having a few last-minute journal entries dump items into these accounts, assigning all journal entries to a single general ledger accountant who is warned not to make such entries will limit the risk of late account changes.

CALCULATE DEPRECIATION

Depreciation is generally one of the last steps in the closing process, because it cannot be completed until the payables ledger is closed and used to update the fixed assets ledger. However, is this really necessary? What if the closing schedule is altered so that the payables ledger updates the fixed assets ledger on the last day or two of the preceding month? By doing so, there is plenty of time to calculate depreciation and post the depreciation entry to the general ledger before the month has been completed.

The main problem is the risk that a fixed asset would be acquired or disposed of during the interval between when the fixed asset ledger was updated and the reporting month closes—a matter of one or two days. Is this difference really important? Fixed assets are depreciated over many years, ranging from three years to more than a decade. Let's take the worst-case scenario and assume that all assets are depreciated in just three years, which would result in the greatest impact on monthly depreciation expense if the first month in which it would be reported is missed. If so, the impact is still only 1/36th of the depreciable portion of the asset cost (which is reduced by its estimated salvage value). Thus, the impact on monthly reported results should be quite small if some depreciation on newly acquired assets is missed.

Where does the missing depreciation go? As long as the fixed asset ledger still shows any late fixed asset acquisitions being entered in the correct month, the depreciation computer program should automatically calculate depreciation for the missing month, which is recorded in the following reporting month along with the regular depreciation for that month. Thus, the depreciation amount is entered twice in the following month for the unrecorded assets, which is usually still such a small amount that the slight negative impact on the financial statements is hardly noticeable.

The only problem with this accelerated approach to recording depreciation is at the fiscal year-end, when the company's auditors may insist on recording depreciation for virtually all assets purchased during the reporting year in order to arrive at a more accurate depreciation figure. If so, this approach is still applicable for 11 months of the year.

The act of accelerating the depreciation calculation shifts two action items into the closing checklist prior to month-end: an early updating of the fixed assets register from the payables register and the calculation of depreciation. These changes are noted in the checklist in Exhibit 4.1.

COMPILE PRELIMINARY COMMISSIONS

The commission expense is one of the most time-consuming and frankly irritating parts of the closing process, because it is subject to the whims of what may be a Byzantine commission plan, including all kinds of splits, allocations, bonus rates, and other adjustments. It also generally begins after all invoices are completed, so commission calculations are compressed into the end of the closing process, just when there is extreme pressure to complete the financial statements.

To reduce the commission clerk's blood pressure on closing day, always begin commission calculations a day or two prior to month-end. Presumably, some invoices were issued prior to month-end, so the commission on each one can easily be calculated in advance and verified with the sales manager. By doing so, only invoices issued at the last minute still require a commission calculation, thereby greatly reducing the volume of work to be completed on closing day.

REVIEW FINANCIAL STATEMENTS FOR ERRORS

The statement review is usually conducted at the last minute, when the accounting department is under a great deal of pressure to issue the financials. Because of time constraints, there is a tendency to overlook smaller errors in the financials and to make temporary fixes to larger errors without really spending the time to thoroughly analyze what caused the problem. Alternatively, some controllers will issue nothing less than perfectly accurate financials and will spend multiple days tediously analyzing every aspect of the financials to ensure that all information is correct.

Either approach can be largely mitigated by conducting a detailed review for errors just *before* the month-end close. At this point, more than 90% of all the monthly transactions will have been recorded, so there is a good chance that numerous errors are waiting to be found and fixed. To do so, skim through the statements to see if any numbers look unusual (in which case a comparison with the preceding month's financial statements is a good way to locate errors). Alternatively, try assigning a complete variance analysis to a financial analyst, in case it seems necessary to make a more detailed review. For either approach, reviewing the statements for errors when you are not in a rush makes it easier to find and correct errors.

Some of the errors found during this early review will not really be errors; they are variances for which some explanation should be provided in the footnotes accompanying the financials. When these arise as part of the review, be sure to write the footnotes at once. By doing so, there is no need to investigate the variances a second time at a later date when completing the footnotes.

COMPLETE SELECTED FINANCIAL REPORTS IN ADVANCE

Recipients of financial reports like to receive selected operational information and statistics in the same reporting package as the financial statements. This is unfortunate for the accounting staff, who must compile the additional information in the midst of the closing process, frequently from nonfinancial systems whose data quality is suspect.

It is likely that some of this information can be collected prior to the closing date, which serves the dual roles of removing the task from the core closing period and also giving the accounting staff more time to verify the accuracy of this information. However, advance work on this area is likely to result in a set of partially completed reports for which some information must still be collected in the midst of other closing activities. Consequently, completing these reports is a two-step process of adding some information prior to the close and filling in the remaining blanks as soon as the other information becomes available.

It is also possible to write selected footnotes and related comments in advance. Although this may involve only updating boilerplate documents and leaving blanks to be filled in later, it is usually possible to write complete text for some variances whose causes have already come to pass prior to month-end.

DEFERRED CLOSING ACTIVITIES

The next few sections describe activities that can be deferred until after the financial statements have been completed.

Defer the Mailing of Invoices

It may seem nonsensical to deliberately delay issuing invoices because this activity interferes with the closing process, especially when month-end invoices (especially in the services industry) tend to be the largest invoices of the month. After all, accountants are aware that issuing invoices quickly results in faster cash receipts from customers—right?

Perhaps not. Invoices issued at month-end certainly have a tendency to be larger than those issued at other times of the month, especially if a job is unfinished and the billing is for all hours worked during the month. However, because month-end invoicing tends to be a rushed affair in the midst of the closing process, there is a high likelihood that some invoices will contain errors, which may take weeks to straighten out with customers. To avoid these payment delays, consider shifting the physical issuance of invoices out of the core closing period and spend more time proofreading them right after the close, thereby eliminating errors and actually accelerating cash flow.

Defer the Invoicing of Rebillable Expenses

If the accounting staff is waiting to close the month because it has not yet received information about expenses that it can rebill to customers, go ahead and create invoices without the rebillable items on the closing day, thereby allowing the closing process to proceed. Do not yet mail the invoices. Instead, wait for the expense information to arrive and then reopen the invoices and modify them to include the expense rebilling information. This two-step process will not affect income statement results, because the rebillable items are first charged to an asset account and then shifted from there onto the invoice, where they subsequently reside in the receivables account—they never pass through the income statement.

Complete Bank Reconciliation Based on Final Bank Statement

Although a recommendation earlier in this chapter vigorously advocated the use of daily bank reconciliations with the use of online bank information, it is still possible that banks will not include all transactional information in their online systems. Specifically, bank service fees and interest income are sometimes excluded. These tend to be small amounts, and so can safely be recorded in the company accounting records after the close is completed and the printed bank statement has arrived in the mail (or in PDF format by e-mail, which is used by many larger banks). The result will be a permanent one-month delay in recording these entries.

Activities Related to Ongoing Improvements in the Closing Process

An additional set of activities related to ongoing process improvements should be delayed until the core closing activities are completed. These activities are described in detail in Chapter 14. For the purposes of providing a reasonably complete list of deferred activities, these additional activities include the calculation and review of metrics related to the closing process, determination of improvement targets for the next month, initiation of programming changes for further improvements, and updating of closing procedures. They are noted at the bottom of Exhibit 4.1.

Defer Nonessential Activities

Defer everything that is not related to the financial close! Too many times, the accounting staff is caught up in utterly nonessential activities during the key closing period, such as attending meetings, going to training classes, creating reports for other departments, or going on vacation. In most cases, it is entirely possible to schedule all nonessential activities so they fall outside of the short period needed to create financial statements. It is helpful to mark "Do Not Disturb" on the accounting department's activities calendar for all closing days. You can even take the concept a step further by putting phones on do-not-disturb status, although this action can impede the receipt of information necessary for the close. The basic point is to instill a mindset not only within the department but also throughout the company that the closing process is a serious affair and requires complete attention during a short but intense period.

If it is still necessary to conduct some unrelated activity during the close, then assign the task to an accounting person who is not involved in closing activities. After other department managers realize that the accounting staff is really and truly not available during the closing period, except by proxy, they will become more amenable to scheduling their requests around this period.

Other specific activities can also be deferred. For example, if any invoices are to be billed during the closing period that apply to the *next* month, do not issue them. Although delaying issuance will result in cash flow problems, taking time out from the closing process to switch to the current reporting month, create the invoices, and then switch the accounting period back to the prior month requires the entire closing team to wait until the invoices have been completed. Also, if anyone creates a transaction intended for the prior period during the interval when the accounting period has been switched to the current month, that transaction must be tracked down, canceled, and reentered in the correct reporting period. In any event, most companies try to jam all possible billable deliveries into the end of the prior month, so there is not usually much invoicing volume to deal with during the closing period.

Altering the Month-End Activities Checklist

All of the preceding timing changes have been incorporated into Exhibit 4.1, which lists all closing activities that have been moved out of the prime closing period, either by accelerating them into the previous month or through deferral. No attempt has been made to slot these accelerated or deferred activities into specific days, because this will vary considerably by company. The main point is to note the volume of activities that no longer must be done during the core closing period.

PRIOR TO MONTH-END:

Review and correct subledger transactions throughout the month

Complete the bank reconciliation every day

Review uncashed checks

Update inventory obsolescence reserve

Determine the lower of cost or market

Calculate overhead allocation bases

Bill recurring invoices

Conduct a preliminary comparison of the shipping log to invoices issued

Review preliminary rebillable expenses

Update the bad debt reserve

Review preliminary billable hours

Accrue interest expense

Determine pension plan funding

Determine flexible spending account funding

Accrue unpaid wages

Accrue unused vacation time

Accrue travel expenses

Reconcile asset and liability accounts

Update the fixed assets register

Calculate depreciation

Compile preliminary commissions

Review financial statements for errors

Complete selected financial reports in advance

DURING CORE CLOSING PERIOD:

Ensure inventory cutoff

Complete all employee/contractor time records

Count and value inventory

Enter late supplier invoices

Complete month-end invoicing

Accrue revenue for unbilled jobs

Accrue commissions on month-end invoicing

Accrue royalties on monthly revenue

Convert division results to reporting currency

Map division results to corporate chart of accounts

Eliminate intercompany transactions

Create and analyze preliminary financial statements

Adjust errors at corporate and division levels

Accrue income tax liability

Finalize and issue financial statements

DEFERRED BEYOND CORE CLOSING PERIOD:

Defer the mailing of invoices

Defer the invoicing of rebillable expenses

Complete bank reconciliation based on final bank statement

Calculate and review closing metrics

Determine improvement targets for next month

Initiate programming changes for further improvements

Update closing procedures

Exhibit 4.1   Closing Schedule Adjusted for Timing Changes

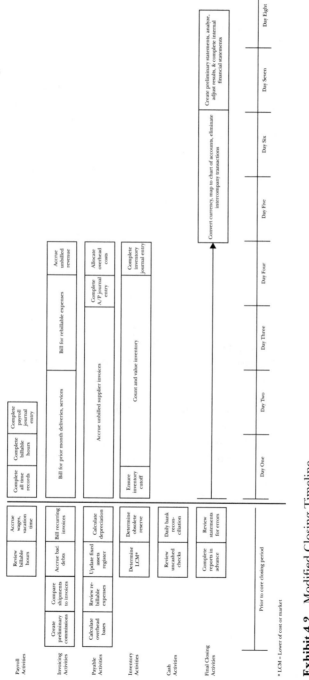

Exhibit 4.2 Modified Closing Timeline

* LCM = Lower of cost or market

This closing checklist can be further refined by specifying the exact dates on which steps are to be completed (even by time of day!), identifying what positions are responsible for completing each step, and incorporating short milestone review points to ensure that the closing is proceeding according to plan. Also consider adding checkboxes to each action item in order to tick off completed steps.

The level of detailed action monitoring implied by this checklist is also a warning to the disorganized controller. Unless you create a closing procedure involving this level of detail and commit to following it every month, the duration of the closing process will not be reduced! If anything, it is more likely to see an initial time reduction immediately following creation of the checklist, followed by a gradual lengthening of the process as the accounting department becomes more slack in its adherence to the schedule. Consequently, it is extremely important to assign overall closing responsibility to a person with a proven track record of attending to and beating deadlines.

SUMMARY

In this chapter, it has been shown that many of the closing tasks can be either completely or partially shifted out of the core closing period. This is a simple yet effective way to create rapid improvements in the duration of the closing period. The impact of these changes is shown in Exhibit 4.2, which shows that the average number of days required to close the books has been reduced by three days from the initial flowchart shown in Chapter 3, from 11 days to 8 days.

Thus far, the focus has been on providing the controller with a cost-free way to improve the closing process while still issuing financial statements identical to what a company's internal and external users have grown accustomed to seeing. In the next chapter, the financial statements are altered in order to strip more work out of the closing process.

5

Revise the Contents of the Financial Statements

To modify the famous President Bill Clinton quote somewhat, "How do you define . . . financial statements?" People tend to include lots of extra operational and financial information in the financial reporting package, which requires much more time to complete the entire package. It is usually possible to reduce the time allotted to the production of financial statements by at least one-half day by stripping some information out of the reporting package. In this chapter, various types of information and the manner in which they are delivered to recipients are discussed to see how this portion of the closing process can be accelerated.

ALTER THE MODE OF REPORT DELIVERY

The controller needs to know what information within the financial reporting package is being read. If some items are being ignored, they are prime candidates for elimination from the package. One approach is to issue a survey to recipients, asking them what information they use. However, what people say and what they actually do are not always the same. A different approach is to post the financial statements on a company intranet site, with each page being separately downloadable. Then notify recipients of where they can go to access the information, and wait for them to download documents. The computer system should be able to track who downloaded which document and when this was done, which gives the controller excellent information about the true need for various documents. Based on this information, it is much more defensible to eliminate some documents from the reporting package.

This approach is useful only for determining which entire documents can be eliminated from the reporting package. To determine the need for individual line items of information within a report, it will still be necessary to survey recipients. Better yet, consider interviewing each person to gather more specific information and additional comments about what information is really needed, which may differ somewhat from the contents of the current reporting package.

This approach also improves the overall speed of reporting delivery, because it is much faster than interoffice mail. The author has had considerable success in converting the reporting package into PDF format and e-mailing it to company officers all over the country.

STANDARDIZE REPORTS

Some departments or divisions like to see their financial statements in a particular layout and may have prevailed upon the controller to provide them with this format. The result is continual restatement of the financials into several different reporting packages, which requires a great deal of additional time. If so, the controller should obtain senior management support in an effort to standardize the format of all financial statements, so that only a single reporting package needs to be prepared. This approach may also reduce the amount of redundant information shown in the reporting package, which may currently have the same information shown in slightly different formats or calculations in the customized packages being sent to different managers.

Because managers may be accustomed to seeing their financial reports in a specific format that is now changing, consider using a mock reporting package as a presentation tool to sell the new concept to managers. Also, if they have valid reasons for altering the new standardized version, be willing to modify it as long as the changes do not significantly increase the time required to issue the reporting package.

If it is not possible to create a single reporting package, then a more complicated approach is to create a Web portal containing a variety of report templates that are linked to a data warehouse in which the financial statements are stored. Authorized users can then use any report template they want in order to download reports in the precise configuration they like to see. This approach has an added benefit: If users can be given the ability to drill down into the data warehouse from the report level to the transaction level, they can learn more about the reasons for financial results without asking the accounting staff for this more detailed information. Furthermore, if users still want to make inquiries of the accounting staff, they can cut and paste information from their drill-down activities into their e-mailed queries; this yields highly precise questions that are much easier for the accounting staff to research and answer.

It is also useful to standardize the reporting metrics contained within the reporting package. Managers have a habit of trying to twist the measurements used to derive key metrics (especially ones involving their bonuses) to enhance the operating results of their areas of responsibility. This can result in a different calculation of the same metric for different managers. To avoid this problem, enlist the support of senior management in deriving a standard set of metric measurements, and then list the details of the calculations in a boilerplate calculations explanation page at the end of the reporting package. If there are still arguments over measurements being used, it can result in reissuance of the entire reporting package. If this seems likely, strip disputed metrics out of the reporting package and deal with them as a separate release of information.

ELIMINATE COST REPORTING FROM THE REPORTING PACKAGE

The most time-consuming and error-prone part of the reporting package is costing reports. It frequently requires the rekeying of data into an electronic spreadsheet, matching it to budget data, and calculating variances, all of which can result in data entry errors. Furthermore, it may not tie to the financial information shown in the reporting package, calling for further reconciliation between the two sets of information. In addition, managers may dispute the variances and do so by requesting further information or restatements of the financial results.

To avoid these problems, recast the cost reports into a separate reporting package that is issued well away from the financial reporting package. Managers will be most amenable to this approach if cost reports are issued more frequently, perhaps weekly. By doing so, the events causing variances will have only just occurred, making it easier to fix their causes on an ongoing basis. For even more accurate costing information, consider assigning the cost accounting staff to operations departments to track daily activity, which accelerates the information feedback loop to company managers.

SEPARATE METRICS FROM THE FINANCIAL REPORTING PACKAGE

Creating metrics for the reporting package can add hours of work to the closing process, because metrics usually require some manual data gathering or calculations. Of particular concern is the amount of user feedback that can arise when metrics are issued, because recipients do not always believe the results and demand a recalculation or reformulation of the underlying equations.

There are several ways to deal with the metrics reporting problem. The simplest approach is to separate the metrics from the standard financial statements, offering to issue them in a separate report whose release is timed to be outside of the core closing period. This approach will be especially amenable to recipients if the metrics are issued more frequently, such as in a weekly report.

An alternative is to still issue metrics with the reporting package, but only for a few metrics that are most crucial to driving the success of the business. This approach eliminates many metrics and the labor required to create them, while also focusing management attention on only the ones that are most critical to company success. To arrive at the best possible short list of key indicators, it is necessary to conduct periodic review sessions with the management team, not only to verify the need for existing metrics but also to see if changes in underlying business conditions will allow for the elimination of some metrics and the addition of others. The most important metrics tend to be a mix of financial and operational measures; examples include the percentage of discounts given to customers, margins by product line, scrap rates, and warranty claims as a percentage of sales.

Yet another approach to the handling of metrics is to permanently remove them from the reporting package, instead posting them on a company intranet site where users can post commentary on the metrics for later perusal by the accounting staff. Other useful features for such a site include a drill-down capability to allow users to determine the detail behind the metrics, and an ad-hoc query capability so they can run additional analyses by themselves. By rapidly posting and updating metrics information, management can more quickly initiate changes to improve the operating and financial results underlying the metrics.

SUMMARY

Clearly, the focus of this chapter was on paring down the contents of the financial reporting package. Although certainly the primary reason for doing so was to reduce the core closing workload, it can also have a side benefit: The resulting mix of reports, online reporting, and more frequent information delivery can actually improve the quality of information being transmitted to managers. It can also improve employee performance, especially if employees are seeing faster turnaround time on operating metrics that are tied to their bonus pay.

6

Optimize the Use of Journal Entries and Chart of Accounts

The use and misuse of journal entries and the related chart of accounts can have a significant impact on the volume of labor required to complete financial statements, as well as the speed with which they are closed. Although their main impact on the total duration of the closing is in the area of final closing activities, it can also significantly affect the time needed to close the accounts payable function.

This chapter describes how to eliminate some journal entries, standardize others, and use recurring entries, as well as how to define and standardize the chart of accounts in order to create a more streamlined and efficient closing process.

ELIMINATE IMMATERIAL JOURNAL ENTRIES

A picky controller who wants perfect financial statements has a tendency to create far too many journal entries to polish up every account, sometimes for extremely small amounts that most people would consider well below the lower limits of materiality. Small journal entries also arise when they were originally created to handle much larger dollar amounts and were never eliminated when the reasons for the entries shrank in size. In either case, immaterial journal entries waste time during the closing process and should be eliminated.

The decision to use a journal entry is quite simple: when in doubt, leave it out. In other words, there must be a clear and discernible improvement in the financial statements as the result of a journal entry.

This approach also applies to the use of accruals to park smaller unrecognized expenses in prepaid asset accounts. It takes time to create the journal entry, prepare a detailed analysis of the asset account, and reverse the entry in a later period when the expense needs to be recognized. In exchange for the immediate recognition of the expense, avoid all of these steps by not making the journal entry in the first place.

STANDARDIZE JOURNAL ENTRIES

Dozens or even hundreds of journal entries can be easily created during a single reporting period. With so many being created, it is difficult to wade through them all to see if the key entries are being made every month and if they are using the same accounts from period to period. If not, the reported financial results will be extremely inconsistent. For example, if a wage accrual entry is made only sporadically, the reported level of wage expense will increase when the entry is used and decline when it is not.

To fix this problem, begin with a standard checklist of journal entries to be completed as part of the closing. The checklist should include a checkbox or space for initials to indicate completion, the approximate timing of the entries, and a reference number to show the name of the journal entry template as it is stored in the accounting system. An example of such a checklist is shown in Exhibit 6.1.

The reference number shown in Exhibit 6.1 uses a two-letter designation for the functional area most closely related to the journal entry, plus a number to indicate the volume of templates within that functional area. For example, the first reference number in the table is IN01, which indicates the first inventory journal entry. Similarly, the last entry in the table is designated GL04, which is the fourth general ledger entry. Some computer systems allow for very large file names, so less cryptic designations can be used.

As just noted, a key part of journal entry standardization is the use of a template. This is a blank journal entry kept in the accounting software,

INITIALS	TIMING	JOURNAL ENTRY	REFERENCE NUMBER
SB	3 days prior	Inventory obsolescence reserve	IN01
SB	3 days prior	Lower of cost or market	IN02
SB	2 days prior	Bad debt reserve	AR01
SB	2 days prior	Interest expense	GL01
SB	2 days prior	Unpaid wages	PR01
SB	2 days prior	Unused vacation time	PR02
SB	1 day prior	Bank reconciliation	CA01
SB	1 day prior	Unbilled supplier invoices	AP01
SB	1 day prior	Overhead allocation	IN03
SB	1 day prior	Depreciation expense	AP02
SB	Closing day	Unbilled revenue	AR02
SB	Closing day	Commission expense	PR03
SB	Closing day	Royalty expense	AP03
SB	Closing day	Income tax liability	GL04

Exhibit 6.1   Journal Entry Checklist

which may be called a template, format, or memorized transaction, depending on the software being used. Users simply go to the journal entry checklist to find the stored name of each template, enter numbers in the template, and save it in the correct accounting period. Templates are intended for any journal entries that are used repetitively for which the account numbers stay the same but the dollar amounts of the entries vary. One should occasionally review the templates to verify that the account numbers listed within them are still correct—a quarterly review is sufficient.

CONVERT TO RECURRING JOURNAL ENTRIES

Most closing processes require the use of some journal entries, and frequently a great many of them. Because some of these entries can be complex, it is highly likely that some account numbers or dollar figures will be entered incorrectly. Another common problem is transposing entries, so debits are recorded as credits, and vice versa. These errors are difficult to spot and always time consuming to correct. If not found, they can significantly affect reported financial results.

One solution is to use the recurring journal entry feature in the accounting software. This allows users to record a journal entry, with all account numbers and dollar figures, and then state the number of accounting periods over which the entry shall be in effect. The system will take matters from there, automatically recording journal entries in succeeding periods until entries have been recorded for the full range of designated months. In the interim, the accounting staff has no work to do, which can make a small dent in the length of the closing process.

The recurring entry is best used for transactions that have no chance of requiring adjustments over the period when they are preloaded to run, such as the amortization of a specific value for a designated period. It can also be used for large journal entries for which some changes are likely each month, but revising the recurring entry is still less time consuming than using a template. An example is a depreciation expense entry for which there are continuing updates to dollar values in the entry based on asset additions and dispositions.

When using recurring entries, it is useful to create a printed list of all such entries and compare it to the entries appearing in the general ledger each month. This step ensures that all recurring entries are running that are supposed to run. Also, consider inspecting in detail any recurring entry that is in its final month of activation. These entries may require slight adjustments so that the total value of a series of recurring entries matches the goal amount. For example, if the objective of a series of recurring entries was to amortize an initial value of $12,003 over 12 months, the monthly entry may have been $1,000, which leaves an extra $3 to adjust in the final recurring entry in order to completely eliminate the initial value.

CENTRALIZE USE OF JOURNAL ENTRIES

It is not especially difficult to learn how to create a journal entry in a company's accounting software program, but this can have the same impact as giving the family car to a teenager with a learner's permit—havoc can ensue. The problem is that more than one person may create a journal entry for the same transaction, resulting in duplicate entries or (if no adequate standard procedure is in place for a closing activity) a cluster of slightly different entries. When this happens, someone must spend time reviewing the journal entry list for duplications, determine which one is correct, and delete the others. Also, if a person making a journal entry does not have adequate accounting training, the entry may be to the wrong accounts or have flipped the debits and credits.

To keep these problems from occurring, one well-trained person should be designated as the general ledger accountant and be solely responsible for all journal entries. If the computer system allows it, consider using passwords to lock out all other users from journal entry activity.

USE JOURNAL ENTRIES TO ACCRUE EXPENSES
DELAYING THE CLOSE

At the end of Chapter 4, the most recent version of the closing process was shown, requiring eight days to complete. A major delaying factor was an estimated three days of waiting for supplier invoices to arrive, so that accounts payable could be fully recorded. It is possible to completely eliminate this waiting period through one of two accrual techniques. The simpler method is to keep a running tally of which supplier invoices are habitually late in arriving each month, and create an accrual for them at month-end. This approach requires cross-checking with the recipients of the goods or services tied to those invoices to verify the quantities being received. If the amount varies, then the accounting staff must make a reasonable estimate of the changed dollar value to accrue in comparison to the prior month's invoice.

The second approach, which is much more accurate, is to require the use of an authorizing purchase order for every purchase over a predefined materiality level. When received, the warehouse staff must check off these items in the online purchasing database as having been received. As soon as this happens, the accounting staff has sufficient information to create an extremely accurate accrual based on the quantity received and the price per unit listed in the purchase order. However, this approach requires more rigorous attention to the purchasing process, as well as access to the purchasing database by the receiving staff.

Another variation on the purchase order approach is to require all contractors billing their hours to the company to use the corporate timekeeping system to record their hours. By doing so, the accounting staff has ready access to all of the labor hour information it needs to record an accurate contractor expense accrual.

Thus, the use of various expense-tracking systems makes it possible to record accurate expense accruals at month-end that eliminate the multiday wait that is traditionally required to receive tardy supplier invoices before closing the books.

AUTOMATE JOURNAL ENTRY POSTINGS

Some accounting systems still require manual intervention to post journal entries and roll subledgers into the general ledger, which adds time to the closing process. The justification for this step is that someone can review the information before it goes into the general ledger, thereby introducing a control point into the closing. However, this step also slows down the closing process.

If the preceding journal entry improvements have been implemented, some journal entries should have disappeared, with most of the remainder being standardized. This should reduce the number of journal entry errors, so the manual posting and roll-up tasks become unnecessary. Many accounting systems contain an option to automate the posting process (which is likely to be the default setting); consider locating this software option and activating it.

USE ACCRUALS ONLY FOR EXTERNAL REPORTING

If a company issues financial statements to the outside world only on a quarterly and annual basis, the management team can elect to not use accruals at all for the other months when no external reports are issued. This approach will result in less accurate financial results for the other reporting months, but if this is acceptable to report recipients, then it can be a valid option. A variation is to designate a few key accruals as still being required for every reporting period (usually any entry whose absence would significantly skew reported results), with selected lesser ones being excluded. For example, if only operating results are issued for some months, avoiding the income tax accrual is a reasonable option, because this is a journal entry unrelated to company operations.

DEFINE ACCOUNTS

If there are several corporate subsidiaries with their own accounting staffs, it is possible that there will be confusion about the use of individual accounts, so the downstream accounting staff may enter numbers into one account that are intended for another account at the corporate level. These definitional problems are not usually caught until the variance analysis stage of the closing process, when there will be a last-minute scramble (and finger pointing) to determine the reason why some accounts seem inordinately high or low, and to use journal entries to shift amounts to the correct corporate accounts.

As an example of account definition problems, a subsidiary may load all third-party engineering labor into an "other expense" account for the in-house engineering department, whereas the corporate controller intends to use that expense to apply for a research and development tax credit, but is looking only in the "research expense" account for this information. This misunderstanding will result in a lost tax credit. Another common problem is when expenses are charged to the wrong account, while the related budget numbers are stored in a different account; this results in significant variances that are too high in one account in comparison to the budget and too low in another.

The solution to this problem lies partially in the use of an accounting dictionary that describes the intended use of each account (also see the chart of accounts standardization solution in the next section). If accountants consult the dictionary when determining which accounts to use for various activities, the odds of making incorrect entries can be reduced. However, because the dictionary is separate from the accounting system and can be lost, review the accounting software and see if there is a way to load the dictionary into the software, so it is more readily accessible.

STANDARDIZE THE CHART OF ACCOUNTS

All of the preceding recommendations can be easily implemented in a few days. This section discusses a much more difficult and lengthy improvement, but one that is necessary in order to improve the speed with which a multidivision company can consolidate its financial information as part of the closing process. A major cause of delays and data entry errors toward the end of the closing process is the mapping of information from each subsidiary's chart of accounts (COA) into the master COA used by corporate headquarters. The differences between the various COAs can be substantial, making the data transference chore a major one. Some companies accept the differences between COAs and create complex automated consolidation mapping systems, but there is still a risk that a mapping from one subsidiary account to a corporate account will be set up incorrectly, creating incorrect financial results. Also, if subsidiaries are allowed to change their COAs at any time, a considerable effort will be needed to continually ensure that the automated consolidation mapping system is keeping up with these changes.

The solution is to adopt a standardized COA for the entire company. This means visiting all of the subsidiaries to determine the need for any variations from a master COA, incorporating these changes if needed, and then creating a company-wide policy to lock down all COAs, with subsequent changes allowed only with permission from the corporate staff. By doing so, the account mapping task is completely eliminated from the list of closing activities, as are any attendant mapping errors. *This is a major improvement for the closing process.*

Standardizing the COA can be particularly difficult to implement if the subsidiary accounting divisions have considerable autonomy or if the baseline COA is extremely large (requiring great effort to pare down). In either case, a good long-term solution is to implement a single ERP system that is used throughout the company, and where access to the COA is locked down and accessible only by the corporate accounting staff.

AUTOMATE ELIMINATIONS OF INTERCOMPANY TRANSACTIONS

The corporate accounting staff of a multidivision company suffers from the unfortunate task of having to back out of its financial statements all transactions going on between its subsidiaries. This can be a highly disorganized effort requiring the skills of Sherlock Holmes and, more important, can also add days to the closing process.

There are several ways around this problem. The most manual approach is to require each subsidiary to add a company code for the receiving entity to each intercompany transaction and then forward this information to corporate headquarters as part of the closing, where the accounting staff sorts through the received transactions and removes them from the corporate general ledger. This process takes time but at least has some semblance of order. A vastly more costly approach is to implement a company-wide ERP system, in which the company code can still be entered with each transaction; the difference is that the computer system can automatically assemble these tagged transactions from all parts of the company, present them in consolidated format to the corporate accounting staff for review, and then automatically eliminate the transactions for consolidated reporting purposes.

SUMMARY

The closing checklist originally described in Chapter 4 has been updated in Appendix A to reflect the continuing need to review and standardize journal entries, which can be completed in the days prior to the core closing period.

The results of all the changes advocated in this chapter are shown in Exhibit 6.2, where the closing timeline last modified in Chapter 4 has now

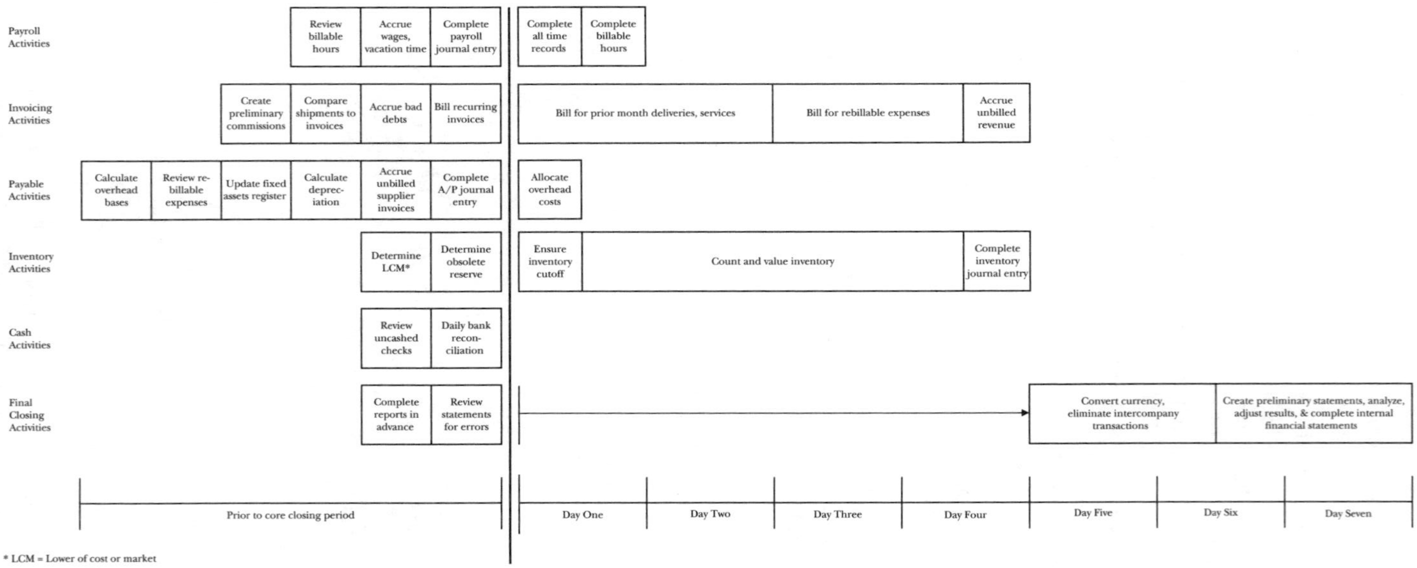

Exhibit 6.2 Modified Closing Timeline

Activity Row	Prior to core closing period	Day One	Day Two	Day Three	Day Four	Day Five	Day Six	Day Seven
Payroll Activities	Calculate overhead bases; Review rebillable expenses; Create preliminary commissions; Review billable hours; Accrue wages, vacation time; Complete payroll journal entry	Complete all time records; Complete billable hours						
Invoicing Activities	Compare shipments to invoices; Accrue bad debts; Bill recurring invoices	Bill for prior month deliveries, services		Bill for rebillable expenses	Accrue unbilled revenue			
Payable Activities	Update fixed assets register; Calculate depreciation; Accrue unbilled supplier invoices; Complete A/P journal entry	Allocate overhead costs						
Inventory Activities	Determine LCM*; Determine obsolete reserve	Ensure inventory cutoff	Count and value inventory		Complete inventory journal entry			
Cash Activities	Review uncashed checks; Daily bank reconciliation							
Final Closing Activities	Complete reports in advance; Review statements for errors					Convert currency, eliminate intercompany transactions		Create preliminary statements, analyze, adjust results, & complete internal financial statements

* LCM = Lower of cost or market

been reduced by one day, from eight to seven working days. The greatest impact of these changes on the total closing schedule was under the "Final Closing Activities" line item, where the time required to map subsidiary COAs to the corporate COA has been removed. The other major change was the complete elimination of the three-day wait for late supplier invoices, using an accrual instead. However, this later item was not part of the bottleneck operation, so the total closing duration declined by only one day.

Chapter 7 addresses the concepts of standardization and centralization, which can create major improvements in the closing process by reducing errors, making detailed transaction information available to the corporate accounting staff for variance analysis, and completely sidestepping the need for intercompany eliminations.

7

Standardization and Centralization

Controllers who have the worst trouble shrinking the length of the closing period are probably those whose companies have many people involved in the process, using different procedures in different locations. These two issues are an insidious and significant reason why some companies never achieve a fast close, because the inherent level of procedural complexity is too high. In this chapter, the need for standardization and centralization within the closing function and how the implementation of these two concepts will contribute to a faster closing process are reviewed.

IMPACT OF STANDARDIZATION ON THE CLOSING PROCESS

One of the most prevalent reasons for a slow close is that the corporate accounting staff must investigate variances and outright errors in the summarized information they receive from divisional accounting staff and spend days correcting them. A problem is often caused by a multitude of different accounting procedures throughout the company, resulting in inconsistent reports that are difficult to reconcile. Also, because different divisions use different accounting systems, it is impossible to spread accounting best practices throughout the company—they may work well in one location, but not in another.

The solution is to implement a common approach to all accounting transactions throughout the company, not just to those transactions that are directly related to the closing process. This approach improves the level of corporate control over transactions. Furthermore, if a recurring transaction error is discovered that presents the risk of significant and ongoing reporting errors, the corporate controller can easily mandate a change in the standard accounting procedures, thereby rolling out critical system changes in a short time period. This drops the corporate risk profile, which is of some importance under the mandates of the Sarbanes-Oxley Act. In addition, this approach improves the level of information accuracy at the source, resulting in far less time being required by the corporate accounting staff to track down and fix errors at the end of the closing process.

By standardizing accounting systems throughout the company, it also becomes much easier to mandate the use of closing schedules and force the accounting departments of subsidiaries to follow them. For example, if a division controller claims that she cannot forward closing information by a scheduled date, she can no longer use as an excuse the presence of a unique step in her divisional closing process—such steps are not allowed. Also, the corporate controller can more easily judge the management talent of the divisional accounting staffs based on their ability to produce financial results in accordance with the closing schedule, because everyone operates under the same guidelines.

An added benefit of company-wide standardization is that every accountant in every division handles transactions in the same way, so it is much easier to cross-train employees, as well as to transfer among locations. In addition, if someone devises a best practice for one location, it can probably be copied throughout the company, because all accounting systems are identical.

Furthermore, standardization eliminates the need for information being rolled in from unrelated subsystems or electronic spreadsheets, which can be time consuming and is more likely to include errors. Instead, the common closing procedure specifies exactly where all data comes from, how it is processed, and where it is posted as part of the closing process. There is no longer a place for unusual sources of information. However, because divisional controllers may adopt their own systems to process data, it is important to dispatch internal auditors to the divisional accounting departments from time to time in order to search for and report on the presence of such systems.

If the corporate controller decides to standardize all accounting procedures, she may simply mandate the use of the procedures being used by a single favorite division. Although this may be the fastest way to standardize systems, it may not result in the most efficient and effective system. If the standardization project has a sufficiently long timeline, it may be useful to analyze the systems in use at all locations in order to selectively pick the best methods from all locations; this approach has the added benefit of probably being supported by more divisional staffs, because they will have had input into the process. Yet another approach to adopting standardized procedures is to base the new common procedures on the dictates of a single accounting computer system that is to be used throughout the company (see the next section). If the accounting system chosen for central use only allows certain procedural flows, then these requirements must be factored into the common accounting procedures.

Given all of these possible approaches, the recommended one is to standardize systems throughout the company as soon as possible without regard for first finding the absolute best system. By doing so, the speed of the financial close is immediately affected. To improve the newly standardized systems from this point onward, create an internal consulting team that regularly recommends system changes based on an analysis of benchmarks, best practices, recurring system errors, and consultant or auditor recommendations.

Whatever approach is used to derive a standardized accounting system, the corporate controller must budget considerable resources to roll out the new system in all locations, preferably first using a single pilot site to ensure that the rollout will work. The implementation will require the use of detailed written procedures with copious examples, training classes, and on-site assistance by qualified staff, followed by internal audit reviews of transactions to ensure that the changes have been properly implemented. Depending on the number of accounting locations, this rollout may require many months of effort.

For more information about the policies and procedures that can be used to standardize accounting transactions, refer to Appendix B.

IMPACT OF CENTRALIZATION ON A MULTILOCATION ACCOUNTING DEPARTMENT

No matter how much standardization is incorporated into the closing process, there will still be labor inefficiencies as well as an increased level of errors if accounting transactions are processed in many company locations. This is because of the inherent difficulty of running operations in multiple locations, the increased number of work queues caused by the involvement of more people, and variations in accounting procedures among locations.

One of the best ways to resolve the closing problems caused by accounting decentralization is to require all accounting transactions to be processed from a central location. By doing so, specific types of transactions (e.g., accounts payable, billings, general ledger) can be concentrated along functional lines with a smaller number of more highly trained people, resulting in fewer errors. Also, by regrouping responsibility for accounting tasks along functional lines rather than geographic ones, it is easier to assign responsibility for various closing tasks to a smaller number of managers, making the closing process easier to monitor.

An added advantage of a centralized accounting system is the ease with which accounting errors can be researched, which reduces the time required to resolve variances in the financial statements. The improvement results from having a single central database of accounting information, allowing financial analysts to more easily drill down through layers of data to locate problem areas. This is a great improvement over a dispersed accounting operation, in which the analysts are forced to ask outlying accounting departments to research issues for them, for which they may wait days to receive an answer. Thus, access to centralized accounting data eliminates the wait time associated with putting variance analysis in the work queues of divisional accounting departments.

The drill-down capability just mentioned is also of increased use to corporate internal auditors, because they can research audit issues much more easily. Also, internal auditors will have a much easier time testing control systems, because more control points are located in the corporate headquarters. This makes compliance with the mandates of the Sarbanes-Oxley Act much less expensive to implement.

Another advantage of a centralized accounting system is the ability to fully automate the elimination of intercompany transactions. Because the corporate accounting staff is responsible for recording all billing transactions, it can flag all sales to related divisions, which the accounting software can then eliminate as part of the closing process. However, because the automatic elimination feature is available only in the most advanced accounting software, the corporate controller may be forced to run a custom report enumerating all intercompany transactions based on the initial flag and then create a manual elimination journal entry. Even this less automated approach is a great advance over the traditional method of manually combing through transactions to find and eliminate intercompany transactions.

The advantages of centralization that have just been enumerated will not be fully realized if the corporate accounting department does not use a single consolidated accounting system. If multiple systems at corporate headquarters require manual interfaces, then the drill-down capability will be severely restricted. Also, different systems have a varying look and feel, making it more difficult to train new employees in their use. Furthermore, software updates to one accounting system may crash any customized interfaces that have been constructed to more easily swap data between systems. For all of these reasons, a single consolidated accounting system is the best foundation for a centralized accounting system.

Another reason to have a single, central accounting system is that more advanced accounting systems contain a workflow management module. Such a module allows the corporate controller to review the status of work tasks within the accounting department. When used as part of the closing process, this can yield measurable improvements in the speed with which the closing process is completed. However, if accounting tasks are being completed throughout a multidivision company, it is very difficult to implement a workflow system in all locations, which eliminates this best practice from consideration in a noncentralized environment.

A good way to implement a conversion of accounting systems from the division level to the corporate level is to gradually do so along functional lines. For example, all payroll activities could be centralized without unduly impacting any other local accounting functions; the same holds true for the cash management and accounts payable functions. Both billings and inventory accounting may require some residual local accounting staff, and so are generally converted last or only partially to a central accounting facility.

There may be highly charged political situations where the corporate controller is not allowed to shift work from an outlying accounting group to the corporate entity. If so, consider measuring that group's ability to issue its financial statements by a specific due date that is necessary for the corporate staff to issue statements by a target due date. If the measurement reveals that the outlying group is unable to do so, or if its reported results contain unacceptable numbers of errors, this can be used as a tool in continuing to request approval for eventually shifting that group's accounting role to the corporate accounting facility.

If it is not possible to centralize all corporate accounting functions, then consider the use of data warehousing in order to gain some of the benefits of transaction centralization. Under this approach, the accounting department of each division uses a custom interface to transmit selected accounting results (possibly down to a fairly detailed transaction level) into a single corporate data repository. There may be an automated error-detection routine in the interface that spots potentially incorrect information and returns it to the applicable division for correction. The corporate accounting staff then uses the data in this warehouse to construct the consolidated financial statements. Although this approach simplifies the reporting process, it does nothing to reduce the error rate of divisional transactions, nor the speed with which it is delivered to the data warehouse. Also, the cost to both construct and maintain a data warehouse is quite high. In particular, if divisional accounting staffs are allowed to alter their charts of accounts, the system interfaces must constantly be revised to map these changes into the proper accounts in the data warehouse.

IMPACT OF CENTRALIZATION ON A SINGLE-LOCATION ACCOUNTING DEPARTMENT

Although the improvement caused by centralization will certainly be noticeable in a multilocation company, it also has an impact within a single-location organization.

In a normal accounting department, closing tasks are handed off from one person to another and yet another. At each handoff, the closing process is lengthened by the wait queue of the person receiving the work. Thus, if tasks must pass through many people, the closing process will be inordinately long. The problem with wait queues can be reduced through a concept called *process centering*. Under this approach, the controller should reduce the number of people involved in the closing, thereby eliminating time wasted while information queues up between people, as well as the risk of work not being done if someone is absent. The decision to centralize closing tasks with fewer people is based on an ongoing analysis of wait times within the closing process; the controller focuses on eliminating from closing tasks any positions creating bottlenecks in the process.

By concentrating closing tasks with fewer people, process centering also allows the controller to have a few people available to work on continuing day-to-day tasks, so the rest of the company doesn't think the accounting department shuts down its normal activities during the closing process.

There is another aspect to centralization within a single location, which involves information flows originating outside of the accounting department. When the closing process depends on the arrival of this information, it is possible that it will be delayed. For example, the billing staff needs shipping information from the shipping department in order to complete final month-end billings. If the shipping information is delayed or inaccurate, this will adversely affect the timing of the closing process. In similar situations where there is dependence on outside information, consider any of the following action items:

- *Control the delivery of information by making an accounting person responsible for ensuring timely delivery.* To use the prior example, this can mean sending an accounting staff person to the shipping department on the morning of the core closing day to pick up and return with all required shipping documentation.

- *Transfer data collection to the accounting staff.* Although unlikely, there may be a few isolated instances where the accounting department can take over data collection, thereby improving both the timeliness and accuracy of the data.

- *Best of all, eliminate the need for the data.* This approach is particularly applicable when *operational* data is being supplied by other departments. Because such data is not usually needed to construct the core financial statements, elimination is a viable option.

INCORPORATING STANDARDIZATION AND CENTRALIZATION INTO ACQUISITION ACTIVITIES

If a company has a habit of regularly acquiring other entities, the corporate controller habitually faces the problem of rolling the financial results of the acquired companies into the consolidated statements. This is a major problem if the acquired companies are allowed to retain their existing accounting systems, because these systems may vary in many respects from those of the rest of the company. There are two ways around this problem. The easiest approach is to create a customized closing checklist for each acquired entity, yielding the types of information needed by the corporate accounting staff. Although this approach allows an acquiree to begin pumping out acceptable accounting information in short order, it will probably require some manual review and error correction by the corporate accounting staff,

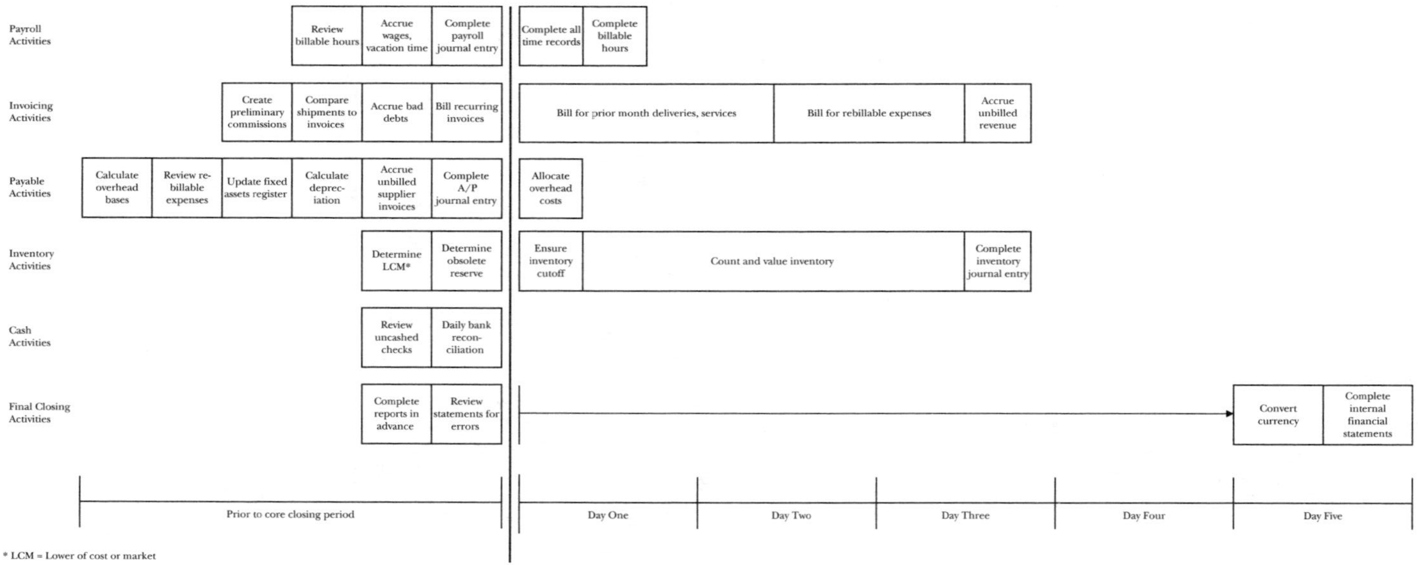

Payroll Activities
- Review billable hours
- Accrue wages, vacation time
- Complete payroll journal entry
- Complete all time records
- Complete billable hours

Invoicing Activities
- Create preliminary commissions
- Compare shipments to invoices
- Bill recurring invoices
- Bill for prior month deliveries, services
- Bill for rebillable expenses
- Accrue unbilled revenue

Payable Activities
- Review re-billable expenses
- Update fixed assets register
- Calculate depreciation
- Accrue bad debts
- Accrue unbilled supplier invoices
- Complete A/P journal entry
- Allocate overhead costs

Inventory Activities
- Calculate overhead bases
- Determine LCM*
- Determine obsolete reserve
- Ensure inventory cutoff
- Count and value inventory
- Complete inventory journal entry

Cash Activities
- Review uncashed checks
- Daily bank reconciliation

Final Closing Activities
- Complete reports in advance
- Review statements for errors
- Convert currency
- Complete internal financial statements

Timeline: Prior to core closing period | Day One | Day Two | Day Three | Day Four | Day Five

* LCM = Lower of cost or market

Exhibit 7.1 Modified Closing Timeline

and so should not be considered a sufficiently efficient long-term approach. A better alternative is to create an acquisition activities checklist that requires an acquiree's accounting staff to convert to the chart of accounts, procedures, and accounting software used by the corporate accounting department. Although this process may call for significant systemic changes by the acquiree, it also results in only a minimal negative impact on the speed with which the company issues its financial statements.

If there is time available for a complete centralization of an acquiree's accounting function, strongly consider doing so. This will involve a considerable amount of short-term disruption, but the acquiring entity will then be in a position to more easily incorporate the accounting transactions of the acquiree into its consolidated financial statements. Given the large amount of work required for such a conversion, it may make sense to hire the services of an experienced consulting firm, although the corporate controller will still have to allocate the full-time resources of several in-house accounting staff members to coordinate and support the effort.

SUMMARY

The standardization and centralization of accounting activities has a major impact on many accounting systems, especially the closing process. It eliminates the wait time associated with variance analysis, reduces or automates the need for intercompany eliminations, and positively affects overall levels of transaction processing efficiency and error rates. These changes are particularly noticeable for multidivision companies with local accounting departments.

As a result of the standardization and centralization actions noted in this chapter, the time required to complete final closing activities has dropped from two and a half days to one day, which (as shown in Exhibit 7.1) reduces the total time period needed to complete closing activities to five days. At this point, there are two remaining major bottlenecks interfering with further reductions in the closing process—inventory and billings. Inventory will be covered in Chapter 8 and billings in Chapter 9.

8

Closing the Inventory Function

Previous versions of the closing schedule have revealed a large and imposing block of time required to count and value the inventory as part of the closing process. In this chapter, two methods for dealing with this problem are reviewed: (1) creating an accurate inventory tracking system combined with cycle counting in order to entirely avoid the month-end physical inventory count; and (2) several ways to shrink the level of on-hand inventory, thereby reducing the risk that the inventory will be incorrectly counted or valued.

In addition, there are discussions of how to systematize the lower of cost or market calculation and updates to the reserve for inventory obsolescence, in order to make these procedures as simple to complete as possible. The chapter concludes with some suggestions for avoiding obsolete inventory entirely, thereby rendering the reserve calculation less important to the accuracy of the financial statements.

CREATE AN INVENTORY TRACKING SYSTEM[1]

A physical inventory count can be eliminated if accurate perpetual inventory records are available. Many steps are required to implement such a system, requiring considerable effort. The controller should evaluate a company's resources prior to embarking on this process to ensure that they are sufficient to set up and maintain this system. This section contains a sequential listing of the steps that must be completed before an accurate system is achieved. This is a difficult implementation to shortcut, because missing any of the following steps will affect the accuracy of the completed system. If a company skips a few steps, it will likely not achieve the requisite high levels of accuracy that it wants and end up having to backtrack and complete those steps later. Consequently, a company should sequentially complete all of the following steps to implement a successful inventory tracking system:

1. *Select and install inventory tracking software.* The primary requirements for this software are that it performs the following functions:

   - *Track transactions.* The software should list the frequency of product usage, which allows the materials manager to determine what inventory quantities should be changed as well as which items are obsolete.

   - *Update records immediately.* The inventory data must always be up-to-date, because production planners must know what is in stock, while cycle counters require access to accurate data. Batch updating of the system is not acceptable.

   - *Report inventory records by location.* Cycle counters need inventory records that are sorted by location in order to more efficiently locate and count the inventory.

2. *Test inventory tracking software.* Create a set of typical records in the new software, and perform a series of transactions to ensure that the software functions properly. In addition, create a large number of records and perform the transactions again, to see if the response time of the system drops significantly. If the software appears to function properly, continue to the next step. Otherwise, fix the problems with the software supplier's assistance, or acquire a different software package.

3. *Revise the rack layout.* It is much easier to move racks prior to installing a perpetual inventory system, because no inventory locations must be changed in the computer system. Create aisles that are wide enough for forklift operation if this is needed for larger storage items, and cluster small parts racks together for easier parts picking. The services of a consultant are useful for arriving at the optimum warehouse configuration.

4. *Create rack locations.* A typical rack location is, for example, A-01-B-01. This means that this location code is located in Aisle A, Rack 1. Within Rack 1, it is located on Level B (numbered from the bottom to the top). Within Level B, it is located in Partition 1. Many companies skip the use of partitions, on the grounds that an aisle-rack-level numbering system will get a stock picker to within a few feet of an inventory item.

   As one progresses down an aisle, the rack numbers should progress in ascending sequence, with the odd rack numbers on the left and the even numbers on the right. Thus, the first rack on the left side of Aisle D is D-01, the first rack on the right is D-02, the second rack on the left is D-03, and so on. This layout allows a stock picker to move down the center of the aisle, efficiently pulling items from stock based on sequential location codes.

5. *Lock the warehouse.* One of the main causes of record inaccuracy is removal of items from the warehouse by outside staff. To stop this removal, all entrances to the warehouse must be locked. Only warehouse personnel should be allowed access to it. All other personnel entering the warehouse should be accompanied by a member of the warehouse staff to prevent the removal of inventory.

6. *Consolidate parts.* To reduce the labor of counting the same item in multiple locations, group common parts into one place. This is not a one-shot process, because it is difficult to combine parts when thousands of them are scattered throughout the warehouse. Expect to repeat this step at intervals, especially when entering location codes in the computer, when it tells you that the part has already been entered for a different location!

7. *Assign part numbers.* Have several experienced personnel verify all part numbers. A mislabeled part is as useless as a missing part, because the computer database will not show that it exists. Mislabeled parts also affect the inventory cost; for example, a mislabeled engine is more expensive than the item represented by its incorrect part number, which may identify it as (for example) a spark plug.

8. *Verify units of measure.* Have several experienced people verify all units of measure. Unless the software allows multiple units of measure to be used, the entire organization must adhere to one unit of measure for each item. For example, the warehouse may desire tape to be counted in rolls, but the engineering department would rather create bills of material with tape measured in inches instead of fractions of rolls. If someone goes into the inventory database to change the unit of measure to suit his or her needs, this will also alter the extended cost of the inventory; for example, when 10 rolls of tape with an extended cost of $10 is altered so that it becomes 10 inches of tape, the cost will drop to a few pennies, even though there are still 10 rolls on the shelf. Consequently, not only must the units of measure be accurate, but the file that stores this information must be kept off-limits.

9. *Pack the parts.* Pack parts into containers, seal the containers, and label them with the part number, unit of measure, and total quantity stored inside. Leave a few parts free for ready use. Only open containers when additional stock is needed. This method allows cycle counters to rapidly verify inventory balances.

10. *Count items.* Count items when there is no significant activity in the warehouse, such as during a weekend. Elaborate cross-checking of the counts, as would be done during a year-end physical inventory

count, is not necessary. It is more important to have the perpetual inventory system operational before the warehouse activity increases again; any errors in the data will be quickly detected during cycle counts and flushed out of the database. The initial counts must include a review of the part number, location, and quantity.

11. *Train the warehouse staff.* The warehouse staff should receive software training immediately before using the system, so that they do not forget how to operate the software. Enter a set of test records into the software, and have the staff simulate all common inventory transactions, such as receipts, picks, and cycle count adjustments.

12. *Enter data into the computer.* Have an experienced data entry person input the location, part number, and quantity into the computer. Once the data has been input, another person should cross-check the entered data against the original data for errors.

13. *Quick-check the data.* Scan the data for errors. If all part numbers have the same number of digits, then look for items that are too long or short. Review location codes to see if inventory is stored in nonexistent racks. Look for units of measure that do not match the part being described. For example, is it logical to have a pint of steel in stock? Also, if item costs are available, print a list of extended costs. Excessive costs typically point to incorrect units of measure. For example, a cost of $1 per box of nails will become $500 in the inventory report if nails are incorrectly listed as individual units. All of these steps help spot the most obvious inventory errors.

14. *Initiate cycle counts.* This topic is covered in considerable detail in the "Implement Cycle Counting" section of this chapter. In brief, print out a portion of the inventory list, sorted by location. Using this report, have the warehouse staff count blocks of the inventory continuously. They should look for accurate part numbers, units of measure, locations, and quantities. The counts should concentrate on high-value or high-use items, although the entire stock should be reviewed regularly. The most important part of this step is to examine why mistakes occur. If a cycle counter finds an error, its cause must be investigated and then corrected, so that the mistake will not occur again. It is also useful to assign specific aisles to cycle counters, which tends to make them more familiar with their assigned inventory and the problems causing specific transactional errors.

15. *Initiate inventory audits.* The inventory should be audited frequently, perhaps as often as once a week. This allows the accountant to track changes in the inventory accuracy level and initiate changes if the accuracy drops below acceptable levels. In addition, frequent audits are an indirect means of telling the staff that inventory accuracy is

important and must be maintained. The minimum acceptable accuracy level is 95%, with an error being a mistaken part number, unit of measure, quantity, or location. This accuracy level is needed to ensure accurate inventory costing, as well as to assist the materials department in planning future inventory purchases. In addition, establish a tolerance level when calculating the inventory accuracy. For example, if the computer record of a box of screws yields a quantity of 100 and the actual count results in 105 screws, then the record is accurate if the tolerance is at least 5% but inaccurate if the tolerance is reduced to 1%. The maximum allowable tolerance should be no higher than 5%, with tighter tolerances being used for high-value or high-use items.

16. *Post results.* Inventory accuracy is a team project, and the warehouse staff feels more involved if the audit results are posted against the results of previous audits. Accuracy percentages should be broken out for the counting area assigned to each cycle counter, so that everyone can see who is doing the best job of reviewing and correcting inventory counts.

17. *Reward the staff.* Accurate inventories save a company thousands of dollars in many ways. This makes it cost effective to encourage the staff to maintain and improve the accuracy level with periodic bonuses that are based on the attainment of higher levels of accuracy with tighter tolerances. Using rewards results in a significant improvement in inventory record accuracy.

The long list of requirements to fulfill before achieving an accurate perpetual inventory system makes it clear that this is not a project that yields immediate results. Unless the inventory is very small or the conversion project is heavily staffed, it is likely that a company faces many months of work before it arrives at the nirvana of an extremely accurate inventory. Consequently, one should set expectations with management that project completion is a considerable ways down the road and that only by making a major investment of time and resources will it be completed.

Despite the major effort needed to implement this system, it is still absolutely necessary as the first step in creating a closing process where there is no need to spend days determining the proper inventory valuation.

IMPLEMENT CYCLE COUNTING[2]

There are two primary reasons for using cycle counting. The main one is to locate the underlying problems causing inventory record accuracy, which typically results in a swarm of transactional errors that have to be fixed before the inventory tracking system will reliably produce accurate records. The second reason is to provide updated inventory balance information that is sufficiently reliable to be the foundation for an immediate inventory valuation as part of the closing process, without any need for a separate physical inventory count.

The following steps show a simplified approach to ensure that a perpetual inventory database is properly cycle counted:

1. Print a portion of the inventory report, sorted by location. Block out a portion of the physical inventory locations shown on the report for cycle counting purposes. An example is shown in Exhibit 8.1.

2. Go to the first physical inventory location to be cycle counted and compare the quantity, location, and part number of each inventory item to what is described for that location in the inventory report. Mark on the report any discrepancies between the on-hand quantity, location, and description for each item.

3. Use the reverse process to ensure that the same information listed for all items on the report matches the items physically appearing in the warehouse location. Note any discrepancies on the report.

4. Verify that the noted discrepancies are not caused by recent inventory transactions that have not yet been logged into the computer system.

5. Correct the inventory database for all remaining errors noted.

6. Calculate the inventory error rate and post it in the warehouse. An example of this report is shown in Exhibit 8.2.

LOCATION	ITEM NO.	DESCRIPTION	U/M	QUANTITY
A-10-C	Q1458	Switch, 120V, 20A	EA	
A-10-C	U1010	Bolt, Zinc, 3 × ¼	EA	
A-10-C	M1458	Screw, Stainless Steel, 2 × 3/8	EA	

Exhibit 8.1 Cycle Counting Report

AISLES	RESPONSIBLE PERSON	2 MONTHS AGO	LAST MONTH	WEEK 1	WEEK 2	WEEK 3	WEEK 4
A-B	Fred P.	82%	86%	85%	84%	82%	87%
C-D	Alain Q.	70%	72%	74%	76%	78%	80%
E-F	Davis L.	61%	64%	67%	70%	73%	76%
G-H	Jeff R.	54%	58%	62%	66%	70%	74%
I-J	Alice R.	12%	17%	22%	27%	32%	37%
K-L	George W.	81%	80%	79%	78%	77%	76%
M-N	Robert T.	50%	60%	65%	70%	80%	90%

Exhibit 8.2 Inventory Accuracy Report

7. Call up a history of inventory transactions for each of the items for which errors were noted, and try to determine the cause of the underlying problem. Investigate each issue and recommend corrective action to the warehouse or materials manager, so the problems do not arise again.

There are several variations on the basic cycle counting system that can be used to make it more efficient. For example, one can split the inventory into ABC categories based on part usage levels, and cycle count the highest-volume A category items the most frequently and C items the least. This approach targets the goal of improving record accuracy, rather than finding underlying transaction problems, which are more likely to be sprinkled throughout the inventory, regardless of each item's ABC designation. This approach can present problems if the cycle counting team is used to the more efficient approach of counting items within specific contiguous bins, which reduces travel time to a minimum. One can still use the ABC approach and minimize travel time if items are physically stored within the warehouse so that all A, B, and C items are stored in separate areas.

A variation on the ABC counting approach is to target only those items that are scheduled for use in the production system. By doing so, a company has a better chance of avoiding stockout conditions that will interfere with scheduled production. However, this ignores other inventory entirely, and so should be supplemented with scheduled counts of all inventory types.

Cycle counters may perform counting work for only a short period of time each day. If so, there is no particular need to schedule counting activities into a specific time block each day. Instead, consider scheduling it for slack periods throughout the shift, so it does not conflict with other activities that may be more time sensitive. However, this approach may not work if transactions are input into the computer system in batches; cycle counting should always be done immediately after a batch update, so the computer records will most closely match actual quantities.

Cycle counting work should be considered a privilege to which the warehouse staff aspires—it requires the best knowledge of parts, transaction flows, and probable errors. Thus, to obtain the best results from cycle counting activities, assign the task only to senior warehouse staff, consider paying extra for this type of work, and train cycle counters in the greatest depth of all the warehouse staff. Conversely, do not use inexperienced people for cycle counting, and absolutely never use people from outside the department who have no experience with inventory systems.

Cycle counters consume a great deal of time tracking down inventory problems, so it is important from an efficiency perspective to set up error tolerance levels for categories of parts. For example, if one purchases large quantities of low-cost fittings that can be readily replenished within a short time period, it may be entirely acceptable to ignore large counting errors, because there is little impact on the company either from a cost perspective or based on its impact on production processes. Conversely, if an item is extremely expensive, is difficult to obtain, or could cripple the manufacturing process by its absence, the tolerance level may be zero. Generally, a tight tolerance is considered to be plus or minus 2%, while a loose tolerance is closer to 5%. However, specific circumstances may mandate tolerances of 0% or well beyond 10%.

Another way to track down inventory errors most efficiently is to direct cycle counters to any item for which the computer system records a negative inventory balance, because there is obviously a correctable problem causing the error. However, some companies try to get away with *only* cycle counting negative or zero inventory balances on the grounds that low on-hand quantities are much easier to count and research; following this approach concentrates counting efforts on a tiny subset of the total inventory and ignores the rest, and so is not recommended.

It is quite difficult to locate underlying problems, even if the computer system helpfully details the complete sequence of historical transactions and the identification of every person making an entry. The trouble is that so many transactions are usually occurring that the person who originally caused the problem may have no idea why he or she made an entry, especially if a few days have passed and many other transactions have arisen in the interim. Consequently, expect to locate the causes of only a small percentage of errors, perhaps in the range of 10% to 20%.

Even if one can spot only a small percentage of the errors, be sure to fix them right away. The reason is that fixing one transactional problem will impact not only the inventory item whose record was incorrect, but also any other inventory items subject to the same type of transaction. Thus, correcting one problem could have a multiplier effect that prevents a large number of identical transactional errors from occurring. Over time, as these problems are fixed, the cycle counters can commit more time to the resolution of a smaller number of problem areas, so the "tough nuts" can eventually be cracked and resolved.

One of the main reasons for record inaccuracy is the lack of responsibility for it. There are many positions in a company that can have a significant impact on record accuracy, such as engineers who create the bill of materials, the receiving staff, everyone in the warehouse, and the production staff who uses the parts. For example, a bill of material, error will cause incorrect quantities or parts to be picked, while the receiving staff can incorrectly log a received quantity into the computer system. Thus, a cycle counter may track a record error to a stock picker, who shifts the blame to the engineering staff who created the bill. The best solution is for senior management to hold the entire group responsible for record accuracy, either with the carrot approach of offering a bonus for fixing the problem or with the stick approach of replacing those people who are not helping to solve the problem.

As the cycle counting team finds and fixes transactional problems, it is also necessary to formally document the problem and its resolution. By doing so, the company gradually compiles a valuable controls document that is exceedingly useful for revising inventory systems, both in terms of further streamlining systems and also to keep the company from making a systemic change for which there is a history of transaction errors.

REDUCE THE AMOUNT OF INVENTORY[3]

Reducing the amount of inventory also reduces the risk of incorrectly counting and valuing it, because even a large error associated with a small inventory investment no longer represents a significant risk of misstating the financial statements. This can be accomplished through a variety of methods involving the assistance of many departments, including marketing, purchasing, materials planning, warehousing, and distribution. Because so many parts of a company are involved in the total inventory investment, it can be extremely difficult to gain sufficient cooperation to effect across-the-board inventory reductions. Instead, it is generally easier to pick through the following list of recommendations and implement only those with the greatest potential success based on the realities of the corporate power structure:

- *Shrink supplier lead times.* Include a reduced delivery time in all requests for quotes. By specifying short lead times up front, a supplier realizes that this is an important criterion for a company and must commit to it before there will even be any discussion of orders. One can also specify the exact date *and time* of expected receipt on the purchase order. By making it clear that the company has a high expectation of receipt within a very narrow time frame, suppliers become more aware of the importance of this issue. This requires considerable cooperation from the purchasing staff, who may be protective of their key suppliers.

- *Purchase from local suppliers.* The purchasing department typically orders in large quantities to reduce the transportation cost per unit shipped. This approach may reduce transport costs but increases the company's inventory investment. The solution is to see if purchasing only from local suppliers reduces the total supplier cost. This does not mean that all faraway suppliers would be immediately terminated, because some may have such an overwhelming cost advantage that any transport distance is worthwhile. However, by shifting to close-by suppliers, the purchasing staff has a much better chance of success in reducing order sizes and increasing the number of deliveries. The end result is a much lower investment in inventory. This requires a change in the purchasing bonus structure, which typically targets only reductions in purchase prices, to a plan addressing the total acquisition and holding cost of inventory.

- *Implement phased supplier deliveries.* When a company places an order, the supplier sometimes imposes a minimum order quantity that may exceed the company's immediate needs, resulting in an investment in excess inventory when the entire minimum quantity is delivered. Although the supplier may impose a minimum *order* quantity, it may be possible to negotiate for a smaller *delivery* quantity, so that smaller quantities are delivered more frequently. This concept works best when the supplier delivers numerous items to the supplier and can still make the same number of delivery runs—just with smaller quantities of more items in each delivery. This concept works best for high-turnover items requiring constant replenishment. This concept can also be a problem for the purchasing staff, which must issue a much higher number of product release authorizations to suppliers than was previously the case.

- *Implement stockless purchasing.* One of the best ways to avoid storing any inventory is to have suppliers deliver goods directly to the production area for immediate inclusion in the manufacturing process. However, this is an advanced concept that requires supplier quality certification, continual communication of production requirements to suppliers, revamped accounts payable processes, and direct supplier access to most parts of the production area.

- *Shift raw materials ownership to suppliers.* Suppliers can deliver goods to the company in whatever quantities they want above a designated minimum, as long as they do not exceed the physical storage area set aside for their use. The company logs these items out of the storage area when it uses them and pays the supplier for the amounts used. This has the obvious impact of eliminating a company's investment in raw materials and shifts the burden of obsolescence to the supplier. In exchange, the supplier obtains a single-source contract with the company, ensuring sales for at least one year and possibly for several, and using a pricing schedule that both parties have agreed to in advance. In addition, the supplier can park extra inventory at the customer location, thereby avoiding the cost of any just-in-time deliveries. This approach has the added transactional impact of eliminating all purchase orders to the supplier, as well as all receiving transactions and cycle counts, while the supplier can avoid making a large number of just-in-time deliveries to the company. This concept generally works best if only a few suppliers are treated in this manner, because management of the process is labor intensive.

- *Drop-ship inventory.* The supplier ships the product directly to the customer, bypassing the company's warehouse entirely. By doing so, all of the transactions and risks of product damage are eliminated. This is the ultimate approach to storing inventory because there is nothing to store. It is an especially attractive option for large items, which would otherwise require special handling and take up considerable space within the warehouse. Unfortunately, drop-shipping is an option only in the minority of situations. Many suppliers are unwilling to ship directly to customers, especially if shipment sizes are smaller than full pallets; issuing small shipments increases a supplier's costs, so the company may have to accept a supplier price increase in exchange for this service. Another problem is the need for new procedures to handle drop shipments. The accounting department must be trained to accept a shipment notification from the supplier, so it can issue an invoice to customers and also have a control point in place for verifying if no shipment notification has been received. Furthermore, the company may not want the customer to know the name of the supplier, because the customer could theoretically purchase the product at a lower price directly from the supplier.

- *Cross-dock inventory*. Items arrive at the receiving dock and are immediately shifted across to a shipping dock for immediate delivery. By doing so, the only inventory transactions are for receiving and shipping, while the only inventory move is from one dock to another. There is no quality review, putaway, or picking transaction at all. Because of these missing transactions, the use of warehouse staff is kept to a minimum. To make cross-docking work, inbound deliveries must have a high enough level of product quality to eliminate the quality assurance review, which would otherwise create a potential delay in the delivery of shipments to customers. Also, there must be excellent control over the timing of inbound deliveries, so the warehouse manager knows exactly when items will arrive. This is especially critical when some parts of a customer order must still be picked, because the picking transaction should be completed just prior to the arrival of a delivery containing the remaining items in a customer order. Furthermore, the computerized warehouse management system must be sufficiently sophisticated to tell the receiving staff that items are to be cross-docked and the number of the shipping dock to which items must be shifted for delivery. Finally, this approach requires several docks, because trailers may have to be kept on-site longer than normal while loads are accumulated from several inbound deliveries.

- *Move inventory to floor stock*. The typical inventory contains a high proportion of small parts, many of which are not stored in easily countable containers and must all be counted during the physical inventory counting process. Furthermore, they can easily represent one-third of the total number of inventory items, which is one-third more costing documentation than the accounting staff wants to track. To avoid these problems, shift the small inventory items out of the warehouse and onto the shop floor, where they are treated (and expensed) as supplies. This approach carries the multiple benefits of requiring far less inventory handling work from the warehouse staff, fewer inventory counts during the physical inventory process, and much less inventory costing work from the accounting staff. In addition, it brings more inventories close to the shop floor, where the production staff appreciates the easier access, as well as not having to go to the parts counter to requisition additional parts. However, be mindful of the danger of issuing a quantity of expensive parts to the shop floor that may quickly disappear, resulting in a significant loss. For these few costly items, it may be better to leave them in the warehouse. Also, a tracking system must be in place on the shop floor, whereby someone can check part bins and quickly determine which parts must be reordered.

- *Schedule smaller production batches.* Traditional cost accounting dictates that the setup costs associated with a production run can be reduced by spreading the cost over the largest possible number of units; therefore, really large batches give the appearance of yielding the lowest per-unit costs, even though they also result in very large amounts of inventory to be stored. Instead, consider accepting a higher per-unit cost by scheduling smaller production batches. The reduced inventory investment and minimized risk of obsolescence usually comfortably offsets the increased per-unit cost.

- *Produce to order rather than to stock.* The most common production planning technique is to produce parts in accordance with a demand forecast. Raw materials are ordered, stocked, and converted into finished goods without there being any customer orders directly tied to the production planning process. This approach inevitably results in excess inventory, because some products may never be sold or will at least sit in the warehouse for a long time before this happens. A possible solution is to authorize production only in response to a direct customer order. When this approach is used, only enough finished goods are produced to fill the order, leaving no finished goods inventory on hand at all, and therefore keeping a company's inventory investment at the lowest possible level. Making this best practice work requires great attention to machine setup reductions, so production runs of as little as one unit can be economically produced. Also, a company must do everything possible to reduce total cycle times, because a customer will not usually wait weeks for a product to be manufactured.

- *Reduce production container sizes.* When an employee completes work on an item, he or she typically places it in a container for transport to the next downstream workstation. That container stays next to the workstation until the employee has completely filled it, at which point it is moved to the next workstation. If the container is a large one, a considerable amount of work-in-process inventory can build up before it is time to move the container. If a great many workstations are in use, each one using the same size container, the total work-in-process created by the size of the container can be considerable. Not only does this represent a significant inventory investment, but there is also a greater risk of scrap losses, because an entire container must be filled with potentially faulty parts before the employee at the next workstation has a chance to review the parts and discover any problems. Simply reducing the size of the containers can mitigate both problems. For example, if every storage container in the production area is cut in half, this automatically reduces the work-in-process level by one-half. The process can theoretically be continued until each container holds just one item or the containers are completely eliminated.

- *Reduce machine setup times.* When a machine requires a substantial amount of time to be switched over to a new configuration for the production of a different part, there is a natural tendency to have very long production runs of the same part in order to spread the cost of the changeover across as many parts as possible. The trouble is that not all of the parts may be needed right away, so this practice tends to fill the warehouse with excess inventory. Also, if the machine was initially set up incorrectly, a large amount of faulty product may be created before anyone notices the error, resulting in a great deal of rework or scrap. The solution is to reduce machine setup times to such an extent that it becomes practical to have production runs of as little as one unit. Besides having very small production runs, this concept also results in greatly reduced scrap, because faulty products will be spotted by the downstream workstation operator at once (assuming a minimal work-in-process buffer between workstations). A large body of knowledge has been accumulated in this area, including the videotaping of a machine changeover session for easier analysis, the use of standardized (and fewer) quick-release fasteners on machine parts, color-coded parts, standardized and prepositioned changeover tools, and so on.

- *Reduce the number of product options.* Design engineers like to offer a wide range of product options from which customers can choose. The assumption is that customers will perceive a company to have a high degree of customer service by offering products in a multitude of variations. The trouble with this approach is the considerable expansion in the number of subassemblies and items that must be kept in stock to deal with the full range of possible variations in product configurations. In many cases, specific configurations are ordered so rarely that inventory must be stored for long periods prior to use; the odds of eventual obsolescence due to nonuse are also high. The solution is to offer customers a greatly reduced set of product options. One can then reduce the number of inventory items kept in stock to those used on a small number of basic offerings. This approach does not mean that customers are offered only a bare-bones product; on the contrary, a fully loaded product is acceptable, but the number of variations from that fully loaded model must be kept low in order to avoid retaining inventory for rarely ordered features. Customer satisfaction levels will still remain high as long as customers can choose from a clustered set of features offering them the choice of minimal extras at a low price, many features at a high price, and just one or two variations between these two extremes.

- *Reduce the number of products.* The sales department loves to shower customers with a broad range of products to fit every possible need. A company can certainly maximize its sales by doing so, but the problem is that it is not maximizing its profits. With an enormous range of product offerings comes a massive investment in finished goods inventory, because many of the products will sell only occasionally but must still be stocked against the possibility of an order. Furthermore, raw materials and subassemblies must be stocked in case more products are needed. In addition, the rates of obsolescence will be higher with more products, because some products will almost certainly be over-produced and will languish in the warehouse for years. The solution is a periodic planned review of the entire range of product offerings, with the intent of eliminating slow-moving items. The accounting staff must be heavily involved in this effort, reporting on sales trends, inventory investment, and direct profits by product. The sales department will resist the reduction on the grounds that sales will be lost, so the company should involve senior management in the process in order to enforce the decision to eliminate products.

- *Delay the order penetration point as long as possible.* When products are configured for specific customers, a company must tag them as belonging to that customer and then set them aside in inventory for delivery to only those customers. If a customer delays, halts, or cancels an order, the company is stuck with this inventory, being forced to either dismantle it, sell it off for a reduced price, or scrap it. No matter which form of disposition is used, the company loses money. Even if a company builds only to stock, it may offer so many product variations that it must retain an enormous variety of finished goods, some of which may never be purchased. When this happens, the same disposition problems (and related lost profits) arise. The solution is to maintain inventories at the highest possible subassembly level for as long as possible and then add the last few product features when a customer order arrives. By doing so, a company can store far fewer product variations. By reducing the number of finished goods product variations in its warehouse, a company can save storage space as well as its investment in inventory, while also reducing its risk of generating a large amount of obsolete inventory. The engineering staff can assist with this best practice by designing as many products as possible to be based on a common set of subassemblies that can be easily reconfigured into as many products as possible. The engineering staff can also redesign existing products to follow this concept, or gradually phase them out with newer designs that accomplish this purpose.

- *Use variable safety stocks for fluctuating demand.* Most materials planning systems include a feature that calculates an adequate safety stock level based on parts usage levels and supplier lead times. If a company experiences a steady level of demand, this approach will yield reliable safety stocks. However, what if demand fluctuates greatly, as is the case for seasonal sales? When this occurs, safety stocks calculated during a low-demand period will result in repeated stockouts, while safety stocks calculated during a high-demand period will result in an excessive inventory investment. Even the midway approach of using a safety stock level based on the average level of demand satisfies no one—still some stockouts during high-usage periods and still too much inventory during low-usage periods. A low-budget solution is to schedule a quarterly review of safety stocks, focusing on those impacting the largest dollar value of inventory, and manually adjust safety stocks at that time. Because the materials management staff rarely has time for such a review, be sure to examine only the highest-investment safety stocks, so the review results in a significant impact on inventory investment and stockout levels in exchange for the minimum amount of staff review time.

- *Focus inventory reduction efforts on high-usage items.* When the directive is handed down to reduce the total company investment in inventory, the materials management staff tends to throw up its hands in dismay and tackle the directive for all the thousands of items in stock. The result is a pitiful effort on a per-unit basis, because the materials management staff can devote only a minor amount of time to this goal. Because of the broad scope of its efforts, the company's inventory investment may not decline at all. A solution is to focus the staff's attention only on the reduction of high-usage items. There are several reasons for doing so. First, by definition, slow-moving items are not going anywhere soon, so the materials management staff would have to wait a long time before the natural ongoing usage of these items will bring about any sort of reduction. Conversely, the turnover speed of high-usage items will cause a rapid inventory reduction in short order. Second, high-usage items represent a small portion of the total items in stock, so the staff can focus on reducing the quantity of far fewer items, resulting in both more attention to fewer items and plenty of leftover time for the staff to complete other tasks.

- *Use overnight delivery from a central location for selected items.* It makes a great deal of sense to store most types of inventory in distribution warehouses strategically located in a company's primary markets or near major customers. By doing so, one can more easily ship products to customers on short notice. However, this approach does not work well for the minority of products having uncertain demand levels. It is impossible for materials planners to estimate how much of these items to stock in each distribution warehouse, so they face the alternatives of frequent stockouts or the expense of an excessive inventory investment (especially for those items having a high unit cost). An inexpensive improvement that resolves this issue is to retain high-value items with uncertain demand levels in a central warehouse and use overnight delivery services to ship them to customers when needed. By doing so, materials planners need to store a large quantity of the items in only one location, rather than several. The cost of overnight delivery services is usually minor in comparison to the saved inventory investment. However, this concept works less well for bulkier items, because express delivery expenses rise dramatically with the size of the shipment. Consequently, one should conduct a cost-benefit analysis to determine the maximum item size beyond which it is impractical to ship items from a central location.

PROPERLY RECORD THE LOWER OF COST OR MARKET RULE[4]

A key aspect of generating an inventory valuation is the concept of the lower of cost or market (LCM). Under this concept, a company is required to recognize an additional expense in its cost of goods sold in the current period for any of its inventory whose replacement cost (subject to certain restrictions) has declined below its carrying cost. If the market value of the inventory subsequently rises back to or above its original carrying cost, its recorded value cannot be increased back to the original carrying amount.

Given the considerable amount of manual calculation required to determine if there is a loss under the LCM rule, few controllers are interested in following its dictates regularly. One of the better approaches to enforcement is to have the Board of Directors formally approve a company policy requiring at least an annual LCM review and to then include this policy in the job description of the controller or inventory accountant. An example of possible policy wording follows:

> Lower of cost or market calculations shall be conducted at least annually for the entire inventory.

This policy may be modified to require more frequent reviews, based on the variability of market rates for various inventory items.

Use this procedure to periodically adjust the inventory valuation for those items whose market value has dropped below their recorded cost.

1. Export the extended inventory valuation report to an electronic spreadsheet. Sort it by declining extended dollar cost, and delete the 80% of inventory items that do not comprise the top 20% of inventory valuation. Sort the remaining 20% of inventory items by either part number or item description. Print the report.
2. Send a copy of the report to the materials manager, with instructions to compare unit costs for each item on the list to market prices, and be sure to mutually agree upon a due date for completion of the review.
3. When the materials management staff has completed its review, meet with the materials manager to go over its results and discuss any major adjustments. Have the materials management staff write down the valuation of selected items in the inventory database whose cost exceeds their market value.
4. Have the accounting staff expense the value of the write down in the accounting records.
5. Write a memo detailing the results of the lower of cost or market calculation. Attach one copy to the journal entry used to write-down the valuation, and issue another copy to the materials manager.

Exhibit 8.3   Lower of Cost or Market Procedure

Even with a policy in place, the LCM calculation is likely to be conducted only at such infrequent intervals that the controller or inventory accountant forgets how the calculation was made in the past. Thus, there is a considerable risk that the calculations will be conducted differently each time, yielding inconsistent results. To avoid this problem, consider including in the accounting procedures manual a clear definition of the calculation to be followed. A sample procedure is shown in Exhibit 8.3.

By implementing a structured approach to the LCM calculation, it is easier to complete it in an efficient and standardized manner. Also, because no direct linkage exists between the month-end close and the need for an LCM review, one can safely schedule it for some part of the year that does not interfere with closing activities.

REVIEWING OBSOLETE INVENTORY[5]

Generally accepted accounting principles (GAAP) state that obsolete inventory must be written off as soon as it is identified. Given the substantial level of interpretation that can be put on the "obsolete inventory" designation, this subject area can clearly have a large adverse impact on profitability. If the risk of obsolescence is high, controllers tend to conduct a review every month as part of the closing process. However, because of the extremely disorganized manner in which this review is conducted, it can seriously interfere with the completion of the close. A better approach is to schedule the obsolescence review for some other part of the month and to adopt any or all of the following methods for streamlining the process:

- *Form a Materials Review Board (MRB).* The MRB is composed of representatives from every department having any interaction with inventory issues, such as accounting, engineering, logistics, and production. By creating this group, one can gather information from all parts of the company regarding which inventory items are truly obsolete and which can still be used.

- *Track old count tags.* The simplest long-term way to find obsolete inventory without the assistance of a computer system is to leave the physical inventory count tags on all inventory items following completion of the annual physical count. The tags taped to any items used during the subsequent year will be thrown away at the time of use, leaving only the oldest unused items still tagged by the end of the year. One can then tour the warehouse and discuss with the MRB each of these items to see if an obsolescence reserve should be created for them. However, tags can fall off or be ripped off inventory items, especially if there is a high level of traffic in nearby bins. Although extra taping will reduce this issue, it is likely that some tag loss will occur over time.

- *Record last date of use.* Even a rudimentary computerized inventory tracking system is likely to record the last date on which a specific part number was removed from the warehouse for production or sale. If so, it is an easy matter to use a report writer to extract and sort this information, resulting in a report listing all inventory, starting with those products with the oldest "last used" date. By sorting the report with the oldest last usage date listed first, one can readily arrive at a sort list of items requiring further investigation for potential obsolescence. However, this approach does not yield sufficient proof that an item will never be used again, because it may be an essential component of an item that has not been scheduled for production in some time or a service part for which demand is low. To avoid this problem, include on the report all planned material usage, which requires a linkage to the materials planning system.

- *Review the "where used" report.* If a computer system includes a bill of materials, there is a strong likelihood that it also generates a "where used" report, listing all the bills of materials for which an inventory item is used. If there is no "where used" listed on the report for an item, it is likely that a part is no longer needed. This report is most effective if bills of materials are removed from the computer system or deactivated as soon as products are withdrawn from the market; this more clearly reveals those inventory items that are no longer needed.

- *Review engineering change orders.* An engineering change order lists those product parts being replaced by different ones, as well as when the changeover is scheduled to take place. One can then search the inventory database to see how many of the parts being replaced are still in stock, which can then be totaled, yielding another variation on the amount of obsolete inventory on hand.

In order to make any of these review systems work, it is necessary to create policies and procedures as well as ongoing scheduled review dates. By doing so, there is a strong likelihood that obsolescence reviews will become a regular part of a company's activities. In particular, consider a Board-mandated policy to conduct at least quarterly obsolescence reviews, which gives management an opportunity to locate items before they become too old to be disposed of at a reasonable price. Another Board policy should state that management will actively seek out and dispose of work-in-process or finished goods with an unacceptable quality level. By doing so, goods are kept from being stored in the warehouse in the first place, so the MRB never has to deal with the issue at a later date.

PREVENTING OBSOLETE INVENTORY[6]

How to review obsolete inventory while not interfering with the monthly close has now been determined, but an even better approach is to have so little obsolete inventory that the recording of an obsolete inventory reserve is rendered nearly irrelevant. Several techniques for doing so are listed in this section.

A major source of obsolete inventory is excessive purchasing volumes. The purchasing department may be purchasing in very large quantities in order to save itself the trouble of issuing a multitude of purchase orders for smaller quantities, or because it can obtain lower prices by purchasing in large volumes. This problem can be avoided through the use of just-in-time purchasing practices, purchasing only those items authorized by a material requirements planning system, or by setting high inventory turnover goals for the materials management department.

A well-run purchasing department will use bills of materials to determine the parts needed to build a product and then order them in the quantities specified in the bills. However, if a bill of material is incorrect, then the items purchased will either be the wrong ones or the correct ones but in the wrong quantities. To avoid this problem, the bill of materials should be audited regularly for accuracy. An additional way to repair bills of materials is to investigate why some kitted items are returned unused to the warehouse or additional items are requested by the production staff. These added transactions usually indicate incorrect bills of materials.

It is easy for a part to become obsolete if no one knows where it is. If it is buried in an odd corner of the warehouse, there is not much chance that it will be used up. To avoid this problem, there should be location codes in the inventory database for every part, along with continual cycle counting to ensure that locations are correct. A periodic audit of location codes will give management a clear view of the accuracy of this information.

When the marketing department investigates the possibility of withdrawing a product from sale, it frequently does so without determining how much inventory of both the finished product and its component parts remain on hand. At most, the marketing staff concerns itself only with clearing out excess finished goods, because this can be readily identified. Those unique parts used only in the manufacture of a withdrawn product will then be left to gather dust in the warehouse and will eventually be sold off as scrap only after a substantial amount of time has passed. To avoid this situation, the engineering, marketing, production, and accounting managers should review all proposed product cancellations to determine how much inventory will be left hanging on the proposed cancellation date. The result may be a revised termination date designed to first clear out all remaining stocks.

A related problem is poor engineering change control. If the engineering department does not verify that old parts are completely used up before installing a new part in a product, the remaining quantities of the old part will be rendered obsolete. To avoid this problem, have the accounting, production, and engineering managers determine the best time to effect the change that will minimize the old stock. Furthermore, if there is an automatic ordering flag in the computer system, shut it off for any items being withdrawn from use through an engineering change order. Otherwise, the system will reorder parts that have been deliberately drawn down below their reorder points.

Some products have limited shelf lives and must be thrown out if they are not used by a certain date. This certainly applies to all food products and can even be an issue with such other items as gaskets and seals, which dry out over time. In a large warehouse with thousands of inventory items and only a small number of these limited-life products, it can be difficult to specially track them and ensure that they will be used prior to their expiration dates. A mix of the following changes must be implemented to ensure proper shelf life control:

- *Record shelf life date in the computer system.* The computer system can record the ending shelf life date for each item in the warehouse. This calls for a special field in the inventory record that is not present in many standard inventory systems, so one must either obtain standard software containing this feature or have the existing database altered to make this feature available. The receiving staff must be warned by the computer system upon the arrival of a limited-shelf-life item, so a flag must also be available in the item master file for this purpose. With both of these software changes in hand, one can use the computer system to warn of impending product obsolescence for specific items.

- *Manually track limited-shelf-life items.* A simpler variation is to still have a flag in the item master file warn of the arrival of limited-shelf-life items, but to then have the warehouse staff manually track the obsolescence problem from that point onward. This means clearly tagging each item with its shelf life date, so anyone picking inventory can clearly see which items must be picked first. Although this is a much less expensive solution, it relies on both the receiving staff and stock pickers to ensure that the oldest items are used first.

- *Use gravity flow racks.* This is a racking system set at a slight downward angle to the picker and containing rollers. Cartons of arriving items are loaded into the back of the rack, where they queue up behind cartons containing older items. Pickers then take the oldest items from the front of the rack. Because of this load-in-back, pick-in-front configuration, inventory is always used in a first-in, first-out manner, ensuring that the oldest items are always used first. This is an excellent way to control item shelf life, because there is no conscious need to pick one item over another in order to use the oldest one first. Similar racking systems are available for pallet-sized loads. However, this system does not absolutely ensure that items will be used prior to their shelf life dates; if there are many items in front of an item in a gravity flow rack, or if demand is minimal, then it still will not be used in time.

If one can identify any of these problems as being the cause of obsolescence, quantify the cost of each problem and aggressively push for any changes that will eliminate them, thereby reducing the significance of the obsolescence reserve as part of the closing process.

SUMMARY

This chapter has shown how to achieve an exceedingly rapid close of the inventory function. Given the number of tasks involved in improving inventory counts, and especially to reduce the overall quantity of inventory to be counted, expect to take at least six months to essentially eliminate inventory from the prime closing period. Because of the high risk of inventory valuation errors in poorly controlled inventory environments, it may be wise to begin improving this area at the beginning of a fast close project, continually improving it while other closing tasks are completed. It is entirely likely that some inventory closing improvements will still be underway when all other fast close opportunities have been implemented.

Although the inventory system improvements recommended in this chapter certainly affect the completion interval needed for the inventory function (see Exhibit 8.4), they do not reduce the overall time required to produce financial statements, because the billing function remains the

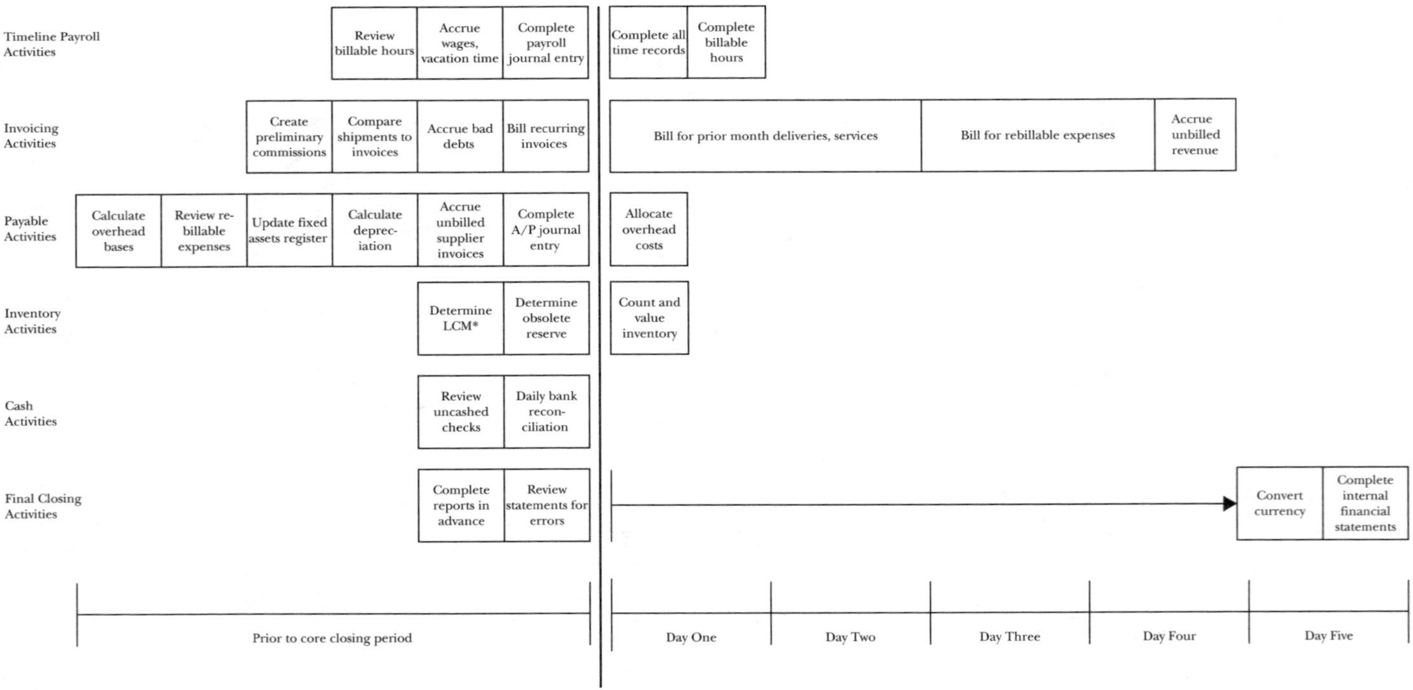

Timeline Payroll Activities: Calculate overhead bases · Review re-billable expenses · Review billable hours · Create preliminary commissions · Compare shipments to invoices · Accrue wages, vacation time · Complete payroll journal entry · Complete all time records · Complete billable hours

Invoicing Activities: Bill recurring invoices · Accrue bad debts · Update fixed assets register · Calculate depreciation · Bill for prior month deliveries, services · Bill for rebillable expenses · Accrue unbilled revenue

Payable Activities: Complete A/P journal entry · Accrue unbilled supplier invoices · Allocate overhead costs

Inventory Activities: Determine obsolete reserve · Determine LCM* · Count and value inventory

Cash Activities: Daily bank reconciliation · Review uncashed checks

Final Closing Activities: Review statements for errors · Complete reports in advance · Convert currency · Complete internal financial statements

Prior to core closing period | Day One | Day Two | Day Three | Day Four | Day Five

* LCM = Lower of cost or market

Exhibit 8.4 Modified Closing Timeline

bottleneck operation. To compress the closing timeline down to the desired target of one day, turn to Chapter 9, which addresses how to compress month-end invoicing activities.

ENDNOTES

1. Adapted with permission from Chapter 14 of Bragg, *Inventory Accounting* (Hoboken, NJ: John Wiley & Sons, Inc., 2005).
2. Ibid.
3. Adapted with permission from Bragg, *Inventory Best Practices* (Hoboken, NJ: John Wiley & Sons, Inc., 2005).
4. Adapted with permission from Chapter 8 of Bragg, *Inventory Accounting* (Hoboken, NJ: John Wiley & Sons, Inc., 2005).
5. Adapted with permission from Chapter 11 of Bragg, *Inventory Accounting* (Hoboken, NJ: John Wiley & Sons, Inc., 2005).
6. Ibid.

9

Closing the Billing Function[1]

As noted at the end of Chapter 8, the last remaining significant bottle-neck in the march toward a fast close is the month-end billing function. The invoicing staff must handle recurring invoices, wait for shipment notifications from the shipping department, wait for the accumulation of billable hours from the payroll department, and wait for the accumulation of rebillable expenses from the accounts payable department, all of which can require several days to receive. This chapter addresses most of these issues, as well as a few more. One billing issue related to the payroll department will be resolved in the next chapter.

BILL RECURRING INVOICES IN THE PRECEDING MONTH

There are many situations in which a company knows the exact amount of a customer billing, well before the date on which the invoice is to be sent. For example, a subscription is for a preset amount, or is a contractual obligation, such as a rent payment. In these cases, it makes sense to create the invoice and deliver it to the customer one or two weeks in advance of the date when it is actually due. By doing so, the invoice has more time to be routed through the receiving organization, passing through the mail room, accounting staff, authorized signatory, and back to the accounts payable staff for payment. This makes it much more likely that the invoice will be paid on time, which improves cash flow and reduces a company's investment in accounts receivable. Of particular importance to this discussion, early billing removes recurring invoice creation from the closing process.

The main difficulty with advance billings is that the date of the invoice should be shifted forward to the accounting period in which the invoice is supposed to be billed. Otherwise, the revenue will be recognized too early, which distorts the financial statements. Shifting the accounting period forward is not difficult for most accounting software systems, but the controller must remember to shift *back* to the current period after the invoice processing has been completed; otherwise, all other current transactions that are subsequently entered will be recorded in the *next* accounting period, rather than the current one.

COMPUTERIZE THE SHIPPING LOG

For a company with no computer linkage to the shipping dock, the typical sequence of events leading up to the creation of an invoice is that copies of the packing slip and the initial customer order form are manually delivered to the accounting department from the shipping dock; then the accounting staff uses this information to create an invoice. Unfortunately, this manual transfer of information can sometimes lead to missing documents, which means that the accounting department does not create an invoice and sales are lost. In addition, this system can be a slow one; if the shipping department is a long way away from the accounting department, perhaps in a different city, it may be several days before the invoice can be created, which increases the time period before a customer will receive the invoice and pay it.

Finally, there is a problem with data entry, because the accounting staff must manually reenter some or all of the customer information before creating an invoice (depending on the amount of data already entered into the computer system by the order entry department). Any additional data entry brings up the risk of incorrect information being entered on an invoice, which may result in collection problems, especially if the data entry error is related to an incorrect shipment quantity. All of these problems will result in multiday delays in the closing process, because there is frequently a spike in month-end shipments that creates a significant backlog of billing work for the accounting department.

The solution to this problem is to provide for the direct entry of shipping information into the corporate computer system by the shipping staff at the shipping location. By doing so, there is no longer any time delay in issuing invoices, nor is there a risk that the accounting staff will incorrectly enter shipping information into an invoice. There is still a risk that the shipping staff will incorrectly enter information, but this is less likely, because they are the ones who shipped the product, and they are most familiar with shipping quantities and other related information. For this system to function properly, there must be a computer terminal in the shipping area that is directly linked to the accounting database. In addition, the shipping staff must be properly trained in how to enter a shipment into the computer. There should also be a continuing internal audit review of the accuracy of the data entered at this location, to ensure that the procedure is continuing to be handled correctly. Finally, the accounting software should have a data input screen allowing the shipping staff to enter shipping information.

These requirements tend to be minor problems at most companies, because there is usually a computer terminal already in or near the shipping area, and most accounting packages are already set up to handle the direct entry of shipping information; some even do so automatically as soon as the shipping staff creates a bill of lading or packing slip through the computer system. In short, unless there are antiquated systems on hand or a poorly trained or unreliable shipping staff, it is not normally a difficult issue to have the shipping employees directly enter shipping information into the accounting system, which can then be used to immediately create and issue invoices. This change has a major impact on the month-end billing process, typically reducing it to just a few hours.

ELIMINATE REBILLABLE EXPENSE PROCESSING FROM THE CORE CLOSING PERIOD

A major delay in the closing process can arise if expenses are being rebilled to customers, because the billings clerk must wait to create invoices until the payables staff has closed the payables ledger and charged expenses to specific billable jobs, which can take multiple days if the payables department manager prefers to wait for all possible supplier invoices from the preceding month to arrive in the mail. Furthermore, some expenses can be rebilled to customers, whereas others must be charged to expense; depending on the level of internal documentation, it may not be immediately clear how to treat expenses, which calls for lengthy internal reviews before related invoices can finally be sent to customers, all of which requires extra time within the closing process.

There are two solutions to this problem. One is to immediately issue invoices to customers for everything but rebillable expenses, thereby removing the rebillable expenses issue from the closing process. This means that all rebillable expenses should be stored in an asset account until they are rebilled, so there is no impact on the income statement if they are not rebilled until several days after the financial statements have been issued. However, this approach may not work if customers want to see a consolidated month-end invoice that includes rebilled expenses.

The second solution resolves the customer concern by recording initial invoices during the core closing period, but not physically issuing the invoices for several days, when the rebillable expense information becomes available. Under this approach, rebillable expenses are stored in an asset account in order to avoid any impact on the income statement; invoices are reopened once all rebillable items have been received, the expenses are added to the invoices as separate line items, and the invoices are then mailed to customers. This approach initially looks as though the accounting department is making retroactive adjustments to the prior period's financial statements, but these changes affect only the balance sheet—expenses are being moved from an asset account to the accounts receivable account. This reallocation between asset accounts in a prior period tends to be minor in proportion to the total balance sheet amount and has no impact on reported revenue or profits, and so may be acceptable to most controllers.

ELIMINATE MONTH-END STATEMENTS

Those employees in charge of printing and issuing invoices each day have another document that they print and issue each month: the month-end statement. This is a listing of all open invoices that customers have not yet paid. Although it seems like a good idea to tell customers what they still owe, the reality of the situation is that most customers throw away their statements without reading them. The printing of month-end statements is sometimes included in the closing checklist, and so interferes with other closing tasks.

The simple approach to eliminating this problem is to stop printing statements. By doing so, one can avoid not only the time and effort of printing the statements but also eliminate the cost of the special form used to print the statements, as well as the cost of stuffing them in envelopes and mailing them. Although it is possible that the collections staff may complain that this collection tool is being taken away from them, it is at best a poor method for bringing in errant accounts receivable and does little to reduce the workload of the collections personnel. If the collections staff's arguments sway the controller to keep this activity, then at least schedule statement printing to occur at some other time than during the core closing period.

PRINT INVOICES EVERY DAY

The accounting departments of smaller companies do not like to issue invoices every day, because there is typically some setup time involved in the process, rendering it inefficient. They prefer to let shipment information pile up for a few days and then periodically create invoices in batches. This can be a serious problem at month-end if several days of invoices have piled up, because it requires yet more time by the billings staff to complete their month-end billing activities.

A possible solution is to force the accounting department to print invoices every day. There will likely be complaints about inefficiency, but this will encourage the accounting department to find the most efficient way to set up the invoicing process. This is akin to the use of rapid setup times in the manufacturing area so that production runs of a single unit become economical.

A variation on this approach for those companies providing labor-related services is to bill on a weekly instead of monthly basis. This requires one to accumulate staff time sheets more frequently and quadruples the amount of billing time required to create four times the number of invoices. The time sheet accumulation problem can be reduced by having employees use the Internet to log into a central timekeeping system, so the billing staff can easily see who has not entered their time and can issue reminders in a timely manner.

TRANSMIT TRANSACTIONS VIA ELECTRONIC DATA INTERCHANGE

Sending an invoice to a customer is a highly labor-intensive process that requires several processing steps and error checking. However, it is possible in a limited number of situations to use electronic data interchange (EDI) to have a company's computer system automatically issue an electronic invoice. This invoice is set up in a standard format (as defined by an international standard-setting organization) and transmitted to a third-party mainframe computer, where it is left in an electronic mailbox. The customer's computer automatically polls this mailbox several times a day and extracts the electronic invoice information. Once received, the format is automatically translated into the invoice format used by the recipient's computer and stored in the accounting system's database for payment. At no time does anyone have to manually handle the data, which eliminates the risk of lost or erroneous invoicing data. This is an excellent approach for those companies that can afford to invest in setting up EDI with their customers, because it fully automates several invoicing steps, resulting in a high degree of efficiency and reliability. Of more importance to this discussion, it can completely eliminate the invoice-creation task from the closing process.

There are several problems with EDI that keep most smaller companies from using it, especially if they have many low-volume customer accounts. The main problem is that it takes time and persuasion to get a customer to agree to use EDI as the basis for receiving invoices. This may take several trips to each customer, including time to send trial transmissions to the customer's computer to ensure that the system works properly. To do this with a large number of low-volume customers is not cost effective, so the practice is generally confined to companies with high-volume customers, involving a great many invoices, so the investment by both parties pays off fairly quickly.

The other problem is that the most efficient EDI systems require some automation. A standard EDI system requires one to manually enter all transactions, as well as manually extract them from the EDI mailbox and keypunch them into the receiving computer. To fully automate the system, a company must have its software engineers program an interface between the accounting computer system and the EDI system, which can be an expensive undertaking. Without the interface, an EDI system is really nothing more than an expensive fax machine. Thus, installing a fully operational EDI system is usually limited to transactions with high-volume customers and requires a considerable programming expense to achieve full automation.

SUMMARY

The net effect of the changes in this chapter on the closing process are significant. As noted in Exhibit 9.1, two days have been removed from the closing process, reducing the total time line to just three and one-half days.

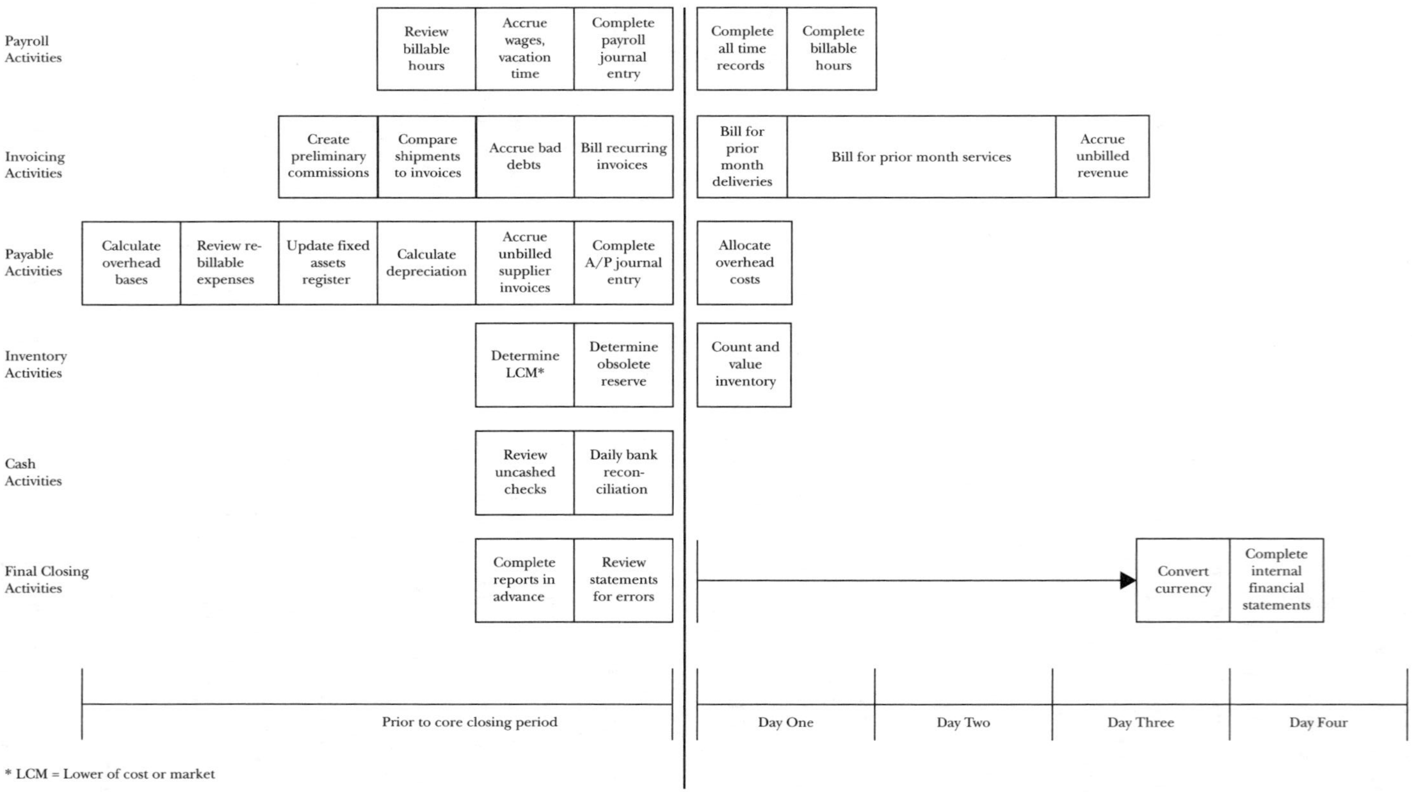

Payroll Activities — Calculate overhead bases · Review re-billable expenses · Create preliminary commissions · Review billable hours · Accrue wages, vacation time · Complete payroll journal entry · Complete all time records · Complete billable hours

Invoicing Activities — Compare shipments to invoices · Accrue bad debts · Bill recurring invoices · Bill for prior month deliveries · Bill for prior month services · Accrue unbilled revenue

Payable Activities — Update fixed assets register · Calculate depreciation · Accrue unbilled supplier invoices · Complete A/P journal entry · Allocate overhead costs

Inventory Activities — Determine LCM* · Determine obsolete reserve · Count and value inventory

Cash Activities — Review uncashed checks · Daily bank reconciliation

Final Closing Activities — Complete reports in advance · Review statements for errors · Convert currency · Complete internal financial statements

Timeline: Prior to core closing period | Day One | Day Two | Day Three | Day Four

* LCM = Lower of cost or market

Exhibit 9.1 Modified Closing Timeline

However, there is still a delay in the billing process caused by the absence of timely information from the payroll department regarding billable employee hours, which also causes a delay in accruing unbilled revenue (which consists mostly of labor hours). These issues are addressed in Chapter 10, which covers payroll-related topics.

ENDNOTE

1. Several sections of this chapter are adapted with permission from Chapters 4 and 5 of Bragg, *Billings and Collections Best Practices* (Hoboken, NJ: John Wiley & Sons, Inc., 2005).

10

Closing the Payroll Function[1]

The collection of billable timekeeping data can interfere with a rapid close, because this information is used in month-end billings and can be difficult to collect in a timely manner. This chapter examines ways to improve the speed of timekeeping data collection, as well as several other issues that can enhance the closing speed of other aspects of the payroll function, including commission calculations, vacation accruals, and sick time accruals.

AUTOMATICALLY CALCULATE COMMISSIONS IN THE COMPUTER SYSTEM

For many commission clerks, the month-end calculation of commissions is not pleasant. Every invoice from the previous month must be assembled and reviewed, with notations on each one regarding which salesperson is paid a commission, the extent of any split commissions, and their amounts. Furthermore, given the volume of invoices and the complexity of calculations, there is almost certainly an error every month, so the sales staff will be sure to pay a visit as soon as the commission checks are released to complain about their payments, which results in additional changes to the payments. The manual nature of the work makes it both tedious and highly prone to error.

The answer is to automate as much of the process as possible by having the computer system do the calculating. This way, the commission clerk has only to scan through the list of invoices assigned to each salesperson and verify that each has the correct salesperson's name listed on it and the correct commission rate charged to it. To make this system work, there must be a provision in the accounting software to record salesperson names and commission rates against invoices—a common feature on even less expensive accounting systems. However, if this feature does not exist, an expensive piece of programming work must be completed before this concept can be implemented. Then the accounting staff must alter its invoicing procedure so that it enters a salesperson's name, initials, or identifying number in the invoicing record for every new invoice. It is very helpful if the data entry screen is altered to require this field to be entered, in order to avoid any missing commissions. Once this procedure is altered, it is an easy matter to run a commissions report at the end of the reporting period and then pay commission checks from it. This is a simple and effective way to eliminate the manual labor and errors associated with the calculation of commissions.

The main problem with using automated commission calculations is that it does not work if the commission system is complex. For example, the typical computer system allows for only a single commission rate and salesperson to be assigned to each invoice. However, many companies have highly varied and detailed commission systems, where the commission rates vary based on a variety of factors, and many invoices have split commissions assigned to several sales staff. In these cases, only custom programming or a return to manual commission calculations will be possible, unless someone can convince the sales manager to adopt a simplified commission structure (see next section). This is rarely possible, because the sales manager is the one who probably created the complicated system and has no intention of seeing it dismantled.

SIMPLIFY THE COMMISSION STRUCTURE

The bane of the accounting department is an overly complex commission structure. When there are a multitude of commission rates, shared rates, special bonuses, and retroactive booster clauses, the commission calculation chore is mind numbing and highly subject to error, which causes further analysis to fix. An example of such a system, based on an actual corporation, is for a company-wide standard commission rate, but with special increased commission rates for certain counties that are considered especially difficult regions in which to sell, except for sales to certain customers, which are the responsibility of the in-house sales staff, who receive a different commission rate. In addition, the commission rate is retroactively increased if later quarterly sales targets are met, and are retroactively increased a second time if the full-year sales goal is reached, with an extra bonus payment if the full-year goal is exceeded by a set percentage. Needless to say, this company went through an endless cycle of commission payment adjustments, some of which were disputed for months afterward. Also, this company had great difficulty closing its books each month.

The concept that resolves this problem is a simplification of the overall commission structure. For example, the previous example can be reduced to a single across-the-board commission rate, with quarterly and annual bonuses if milestone targets are reached. Although an obvious solution and one that can greatly reduce the work of the accounting staff, it is implemented only with the greatest difficulty because the sales manager must approve the new system and rarely does so. The reason is that the sales manager probably created the convoluted commissions system in the first place and feels that it is a good one for motivating the sales staff. In this situation, the matter may have to go to a higher authority for approval, although this irritates the sales manager. A better and more politically correct variation is to persuade the sales manager to adopt a midway solution that leaves both parties partially satisfied. In the long run, as new people move into the sales manager position, there may still be opportunities to more completely simplify the commission structure. Eventually, this will reduce the time required for the payroll section of the closing process.

INSTALL INCENTIVE COMPENSATION MANAGEMENT SOFTWARE

Commission tracking for a large number of salespeople is an exceedingly complex chore, especially when there are multiple sales plans with a variety of splits, bonuses, overrides, caps, hurdles, guaranteed payments, and commission rates. This task typically requires a massive amount of accounting staff time manipulating electronic spreadsheets and is highly error-prone. The preceding two best practices in this chapter are designed to *simplify* the commission calculation structure in order to reduce the amount of closing effort. However, an automated alternative is available that allows the sales manager to retain a high degree of commission plan complexity while minimizing the manual calculation labor of the accounting staff.

The solution is to install incentive compensation management software such as is offered by Synygy and Callidus Software. It is a separate package from the accounting software and requires a custom data feed from the accounting database, using the incoming data to build complex data tracking models that churn out exactly what each salesperson is to be paid, along with a commission statement. The best packages also allow for the "what if" modeling of different commission plan scenarios, as well as the construction of customized commission plans that are precisely tailored to a company's needs, and can also deliver commission results to salespeople over the Internet. The trouble with this best practice is its cost. The software is expensive and also requires consulting labor to develop a data link between the main accounting database and the new software. Thus, it is a cost-effective solution only for those organizations with at least 100 salespeople.

POST COMMISSION PAYMENTS ON THE COMPANY INTRANET

A sales staff whose pay structure is heavily skewed in favor of commission payments, rather than salaries, will probably hound the accounting staff at month-end to see what their commission payments will be. This comes at the time of the month when the accounting staff is trying to close the accounting books, and so increases their workload at the worst possible time of the month. However, by creating a linkage between the accounting database and a company's intranet site, it is possible to shift this information directly to a Web page where the sales staff can view it at any time without involving the accounting staff.

There are two ways to post the commission information. One is to wait until all commission-related calculations have been completed at month-end and then either manually dump the data into a hypertext markup language (HTML) format for posting to a Web page or else run a batch program that does so automatically. Either approach will give the sales staff a complete set of information about their commissions. However, this approach still requires some manual effort at month-end (even if only for a few minutes while a batch program runs).

An alternative approach is to create a direct interface between the accounting database and the Web page, so that commissions are updated constantly, including grand totals for each commission payment period. By using this approach, the accounting staff has virtually no work to do in conveying information to the sales staff. In addition, sales personnel can check their commissions at any time of the month and call the accounting staff with their concerns right away; this is a great improvement, because problems can be spotted and fixed at once, rather than waiting until the closing period to correct them.

No matter which method is used for posting commission information, a password system will be needed, because this is highly personal payroll-related information. A reminder program should be built into the system, so the sales staff is forced to alter their passwords regularly, thereby reducing the risk of outside access to this information.

An extremely simple variation on the concept of distributing commission calculations to the sales staff is to convert the calculation worksheet into an Adobe Acrobat portable document file (PDF) format (so the calculations cannot be altered by a salesperson), and then e-mailing the PDF file to the sales staff. This can even be done a day or two prior to month-end, so the sales staff can review the preliminary calculations for most monthly invoices and respond with corrections that can be made prior to the core closing period.

AVOID ADJUSTING PRELIMINARY COMMISSION ACCRUAL CALCULATIONS

If a company has several salespeople who frequently share commissions through a variety of split commission deals, there is a very high likelihood that the initial commission calculations put together by the accounting staff will incorrectly allocate commissions, which requires a second iteration before there is a correct allocation of the commission expense by person. However, the process of determining the correct allocation is a slow one, frequently requiring the input of the sales manager, who may not be available at the precise point during the core closing period when his or her input is required. Thus, developing a proper commission allocation can significantly interfere with the closing process.

A simple way to avoid this problem is to not worry about it, because the initial total commission accrual is probably very close to what the final commission accrual will be after all allocations have been made among the sales staff; in short, the commission on each sale stays the same, with the only issue being who receives the payment. Thus, there is no need to adjust the initial commission accrual.

USE A BAR-CODED TIME CLOCK

The single most labor-intensive closing task in the payroll area is collecting hours worked for hourly employees. To do so, an accounting clerk must collect all of the employee time cards for the most recently completed payroll period, manually add up the hours listed on the cards, and research missing hours with supervisors. This is a lengthy process and usually has a high error rate, because of the large percentage of missing start or stop times on most time cards. The errors are usually found by employees as soon as they are paid, resulting in a loud and (sometimes) boisterous visit to the payroll department, demanding an immediate adjustment to the paid amount with a manual paycheck. This disrupts the payroll department during the closing period and introduces additional inefficiencies to the process.

A common solution to these problems is to install a computerized time clock. This is a clock that requires an employee to swipe an employee-specific plastic card through the clock. The card is encoded with an employee-identifying number, using either a bar code or a magnetic stripe. Once the swipe occurs, the clock automatically stores the date and time and downloads this data upon request to the payroll department's computer, where special software automatically calculates hours worked and highlights any problems for additional research (such as missed swipes). Many such clocks can be installed throughout a large facility, or at outlying locations, so that employees can conveniently record their time, no matter where they may be. The more advanced clocks also track the time periods when employees are supposed to arrive and leave and require a supervisor's password for card swipes outside of that time period; this feature allows for greater control over employee work hours. Many of these systems also issue absence reports at any time, so that supervisors can easily tell who has not shown up for work. Thus, an automated time clock eliminates much low-end clerical work, while providing new management tools for supervisors.

Before purchasing a bar-coded time clock, it is important to recognize its limitations. The most important one is cost: This type of clock usually costs $2,000 to $3,000, or can be leased for several hundred dollars per month. If several clocks are needed, this can add up to a substantial investment. In addition, outlying time clocks that must download their information to a computer at a distant location require their own phone lines, which represents an additional monthly payment to the phone company. There may also be a fee for using the software on the central computer that summarizes all of the incoming payroll information. Given these costs, it is most common for bar-coded time clocks to be used only in those situations where there are so many hourly employees in a company that there is a significant time savings in the payroll department resulting from their installation.

A key flaw of the bar-coded time clock is that employees can use each other's cards to clock themselves in, resulting in payments for time worked to employees who may not have even been on the premises. To avoid this problem, one can install an Internet camera next to the clock that snaps an image for each card swipe made and stores it elsewhere for easy access by the payroll staff. The information can be stored for a few weeks in this manner until there is no need for the information and is then written over. By using this approach, employees will be much less inclined to clock in or out for their co-workers, while the payroll staff will have ready evidence of improper card swipes. The main problem with this approach is the difficulty of linking information from the card swipe to the image created by the camera, so one can tell what information was entered into the system by each person.

USE A WEB-BASED TIMEKEEPING SYSTEM

Although a bar-coded time clock will allow a single-location company to reliably compile accurate labor hour information by month-end, this level of efficiency does not apply to those companies whose employees operate outside company premises. In particular, companies whose employees act as consultants or service technicians can have a terrible time accumulating the labor hours of their employees, which must be completed before their hours can be billed to customers.

An excellent solution is to either create or pay for the services of a Web-based timekeeping system (offered by all of the major payroll processing companies). Employees can enter their time into such a system from any computer with Web access. The author's company has created its own Web-based system, which even automatically e-mails reminder messages to employees if they have not entered their time records for the most recent week.

Unfortunately, despite automated prompting, people operating outside the company premises have an independent mindset and do not necessarily place time sheet data entry at the top of their priority lists. Thus, even though the technology is at their fingertips to complete their time records by month-end, they still do not do so. There are several ways to deal with this issue:

- Provide up-front training when employees are hired, emphasizing the need for prompt updates to timekeeping records.

- Issue an e-mail to all employees on the day before the month-end close, reminding them to have all time records for the month completed by the commencement of billing activities on the following morning.

- Hound employees at the end of each week to update their weekly time records. By creating a mindset every week that time records must be updated, fewer employees will need reminding at month-end. This has the side benefit of creating accurate records for all weeks in the month, except for the last one, well before closing activities begin. This is the single most effective way to ensure prompt time record updates.

AUTOMATE VACATION ACCRUALS

The topic that is of the most interest to the most employees is how much vacation time they have left. In most companies, this information is kept manually by the payroll staff, so employees troop down to the payroll department once a month (and more frequently during the prime summer vacation months!) to see how much vacation time they have left to use. When employees are constantly arriving to find out this information, it is a major interruption to the payroll staff, because it happens at all times of the day, never allowing them to settle down into a comfortable work routine. If many employees want to know about their vacation time, the requests can be a considerable loss of efficiency for the payroll staff.

A simple way to keep employees from bothering the payroll department is to include the vacation accrual in employee paychecks. The information appears on the payroll stub and shows the annual amount of accrued vacation, net of any used time. By feeding this information to employees in every paycheck, there is no need for them to inquire about it in the payroll office, eliminating a major hindrance. However, there are several points to consider before automating vacation accruals. First, the payroll system must be equipped with a vacation accrual calculation option. If not, the software must be modified with custom programming to allow for the calculation and presentation of this information, which may cost more to implement than the projected efficiency savings. Another problem is that the accrual system must be set up properly for each employee when it is originally installed or there will be many outraged employees crowding into the payroll office, causing more disruption than was the case before.

This start-up problem is caused by having employees with different numbers of days of vacation allowed per year, as well as some with carryover vacation from the previous year. If this information is not accurately reflected in the automated vacation accrual system when it is implemented, employees will hasten to the payroll area to have this problem corrected at once. Another issue is that the accruals must be adjusted over time to reflect changes in the length of earned employee vacation periods, which may again cause employees to interrupt the payroll staff. For example, an employee may switch from two to three weeks of allowed vacation at the fifth anniversary of his or her hiring. The payroll department must have a schedule of when this person's vacation accrual amount changes to the three-week level, or the employee will complain about it. If these problems can be overcome, using automated vacation accruals can improve the efficiency of the payroll department.

The author's company has taken a Web-based approach to the vacation tracking problem, creating a customer vacation tracking application that is directly linked to our Web-based timekeeping system. Employees log into the system and enter the effective date through which they want to determine their vacation accrual. The system responds with a listing of hours carried forward from the previous year, hours accrued through the effective date, hours used, and hours available. As a result, the payroll department is completely removed from the vacation accrual tracking business.

MERGE SICK TIME INTO VACATION TIME

Many companies have adopted a separate sick time policy for their employees, which allows for different accrual provisions from their vacation time policy, as well as differing year-end carryforward allowances. In some cases (especially in governments), the sick time carryforward provision may be so generous that the controller must accrue for literally months of unused sick time for each employee. This represents a major accrual and therefore a significant time expenditure within the core closing period to generate an accurate sick time accrual.

This accrual can be completely eliminated by merging the sick time policy into the vacation policy. Although the result is likely to be a larger vacation accrual, the avoidance of a separate calculation can save time during the closing process. However, this change in policy may be opposed by any unions operating in company locations, whose contracts may specify the existence of a sick time provision in the employee manual. If so, consider using identical benefit terms for both the vacation and sick time policies so the accrual calculations can be merged, even if the benefits remain separated in the employee manual.

CAP THE AMOUNT OF VACATION TIME TO BE CARRIED FORWARD

If a company has a large number of employees and the amount of vacation time accrued by employees is substantial, then the controller must devote a significant amount of time each month to the derivation of an accurate vacation accrual. For the best accuracy, this involves waiting until

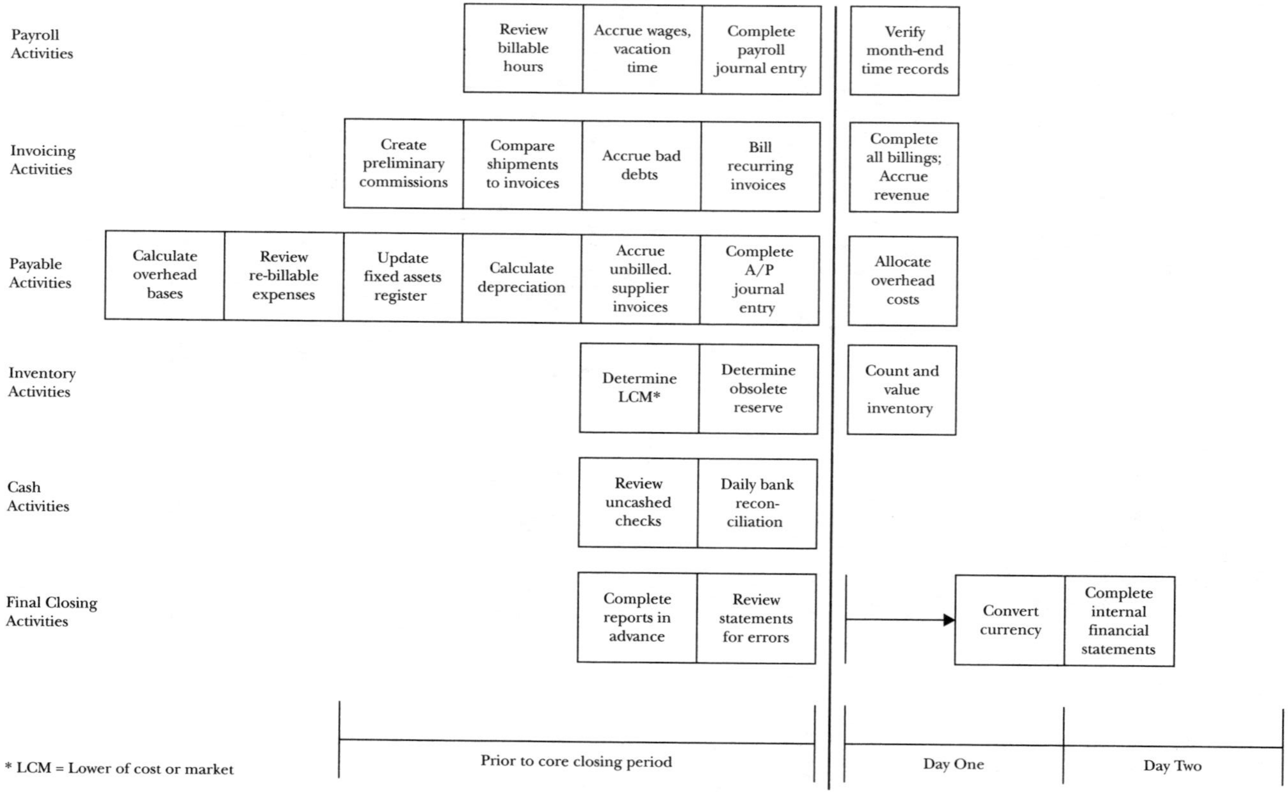

Payroll Activities: Calculate overhead bases · Review re-billable expenses · Create preliminary commissions · Review billable hours · Accrue wages, vacation time · Complete payroll journal entry · Verify month-end time records

Invoicing Activities: Compare shipments to invoices · Accrue bad debts · Bill recurring invoices · Complete all billings; Accrue revenue

Payable Activities: Update fixed assets register · Calculate depreciation · Accrue unbilled supplier invoices · Complete A/P journal entry · Allocate overhead costs

Inventory Activities: Determine LCM* · Determine obsolete reserve · Count and value inventory

Cash Activities: Review uncashed checks · Daily bank reconciliation

Final Closing Activities: Complete reports in advance · Review statements for errors · Convert currency · Complete internal financial statements

Timeline: Prior to core closing period · Day One · Day Two

* LCM = Lower of cost or market

Exhibit 10.1 Modified Closing Timeline

the month is over, then compiling vacation hours taken during the month, subtracting this from earned vacation time, and arriving at a month-end balance of earned vacation time available. However, because this approach depends on waiting until all vacation time has been reported by employees at month-end, the task falls squarely into the core closing period.

A better approach is to cap the amount of vacation time that employees are allowed to carry forward at the end of each calendar year. By doing so, the controller no longer has to worry about accruing for excessively large earned vacation balances, because he or she knows that the balance will be reduced to the cap level at year-end. For example, if a company caps the vacation carryforward at 40 hours, the maximum vacation accrual can be defaulted to 40 hours. In many cases, it is sufficient to simply accrue 40 hours of vacation time for each employee at the *beginning* of the year, and then adjust this balance downward at the end of the year if any employees have used up more hours than will result in a 40-hour carryforward. During the intervening months, there is no need to track vacation time at all or to adjust the accrued vacation expense account, thereby removing this task from the core closing period.

SUMMARY

In this chapter, a variety of techniques were used not only to reduce the overall time required to process payroll transactions, but also to drastically shrink the hours needed to complete month-end payroll tasks during the core closing period. Although Exhibit 10.1 shows that the verification of month-end time records has now been reduced to a four-hour time block on the morning of the first closing day, this should really require only about one hour (the minimum time block in the table is four hours). Once this important step is complete, final month-end invoicing can commence and should be completed a few hours later. The result is a closing period that has now been reduced to only one and a half days.

The final remaining process standing in the way of a one-day close is currency conversion, which applies only to those organizations having international operations. That problem is dealt with in Chapter 13. However, several minor efficiency improvements have not yet been dealt with in two other functional areas: payables and cash processing. These subjects are addressed in Chapters 11 and 12.

ENDNOTE

1. Some sections of this chapter were adapted with permission from Chapters 8 and 17 of Bragg, *Accounting Best Practices*, 5th Edition (Hoboken, NJ: John Wiley & Sons, Inc., 2007).

11

Closing the Payables Function[1]

This chapter contains several suggestions for improving the efficiency of the accounts payable function. Although only the first item (automate the month-end cutoff) has a direct impact on the closing process, all of the concepts in this chapter are designed to improve the efficiency of the payables process. Because payables is one of the most labor-intensive functions in the accounting department, reduced effort in this area can have a secondary impact on the speed of the closing process. The chapter covers such topics as reduced labor in the document matching process, eliminating payment approvals, avoiding invoice payments with procurement cards, reducing data entry labor, and automating the payment process.

AUTOMATE THE MONTH-END CUTOFF

A standard task item on the month-end closing list is to coordinate a cutoff of incoming goods at month-end. This involves segregating all receipts subsequent to month-end, so they are not included in the month-end inventory count. Also, other miscellaneous receipts are segregated so their associated expenses are not incorrectly recorded in the wrong month. This cutoff task requires a considerable amount of communication with the receiving department, frequently resulting in problems recording expenses in the proper month when the procedure is forgotten or ignored. It is also a problem for those people waiting to receive items that have arrived but that are segregated and have not yet been entered into the computer system as having been officially received.

It is possible to completely ignore the cutoff procedure by requiring the receiving staff to enter all receipts into a computer that is accessible by the accounting system. As long as the receiving staff makes its entries in a timely manner and the computer system date-stamps all receipts, it is easy to determine which receipts fall on either side of the cutoff date. The system should also generate a report listing the items received prior to the month-end cutoff date; if this report can be linked to the purchase order database, it may also be possible to include the extended cost of each received item on the report, which is ideal information for accruing an expense for any received items for which no supplier invoice has yet been received.

It may be necessary to have the internal audit staff occasionally review the timeliness of these entries by the receiving staff to verify that they are being entered in the correct accounting period.

This is a simplified version of the next payables improvement concept, which takes the receiving data entry concept a step further, to largely remove the accounting department from the payables matching process.

PAY BASED ON RECEIVING APPROVAL ONLY

The accounts payable process is one of the most convoluted of all the processes that a company can adopt, irrespective of the department. First, it requires the collection of information from multiple departments—purchase orders from the purchasing department, invoices from suppliers, and receiving documents from the receiving department. The process then involves matching these documents, which frequently contain exceptions, and then tracking down someone either to approve exceptions or at least to sign the check paying for the received items, which must then be mailed to suppliers. The key to success in this area is to thoroughly reengineer the entire process by eliminating the paperwork, the multiple sources of information, and the additional approvals. The only improvement concept that truly addresses the underlying problems of the accounts payable process is paying based on receiving approval.

To pay based on receipt, one must first do away with the concept of having an accounts payable staff that performs the traditional matching process. Instead, the receiving staff checks to see if there is a purchase order at the time of receipt. If there is, the computer system automatically pays the supplier. Sounds simple? It is not. A company must have several features installed before the concept will function properly. The main issue is having a computer terminal at the receiving dock. When a supplier shipment arrives, a receiving person takes the purchase order number and quantity received from the shipping documentation and punches it into the computer. The computer system checks against an online database of open purchase orders to see if the shipment was authorized. If so, the system automatically schedules a payment to the supplier based on the purchase order price, which can be sent by wire transfer. If the purchase order number is not in the database, or if there is no purchase order number on the shipping documentation, the shipment is rejected at the receiving dock. Note that the accounts payable staff takes no part whatsoever in this process—everything has been shifted to a simple step at the receiving location. The process is shown graphically in Exhibit 11.1.

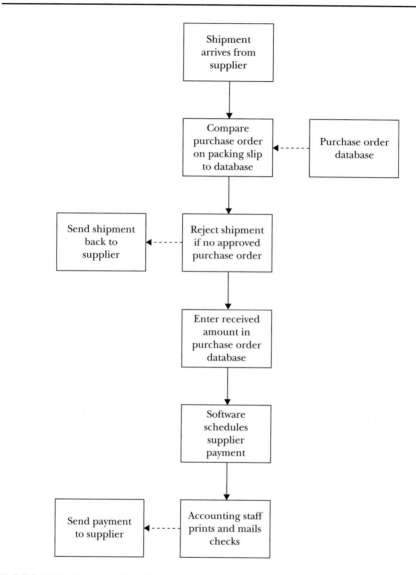

Exhibit 11.1   Process Flow for Payment Based on Receiving Approval

Before laying off the entire accounts payable staff and acquiring such a system, there are a few problems to overcome, as follows:

- *Train suppliers.* Every supplier who sends anything to a company must be trained to include the purchase order number, the company's part number, and the quantity shipped on the shipping documentation, so this information can be punched into the computer at the receiving location. The information can be encoded as bar codes to make the data entry task easier for the receiving employees. Training a supplier may be difficult, especially if the company only purchases a small quantity of goods from the supplier. To make it worthwhile for the supplier to go to this extra effort, it may be necessary to concentrate purchases with a smaller number of suppliers to give each one a significant volume of orders.

- *Alter the accounting system.* The traditional accounting software is not designed to allow approvals at the receiving dock. Accordingly, a company will have to reprogram the system to allow the reengineered process to be performed. This can be an exceptionally major undertaking, especially if the software is constantly being upgraded by the supplier, because every upgrade will wipe out any custom programming that the company may have created.

- *Prepare for miscellaneous payments.* The accounts payable department will not really go away because there will always be stray supplier invoices of various kinds arriving for payment that cannot possibly go through the receiving dock, such as subscription payments, utility bills, and repair invoices. Accordingly, the old payments system must still be maintained, although at a greatly reduced level, to handle these items.

- *Pay without a supplier invoice.* One of the key aspects of the reengineered process is paying based on the information in the purchase order, rather than the information in the supplier's invoice. To do so, one must have a database of all the tax rates that every supplier would charge, so the company's computer system can automatically include these taxes in the invoice payments. Also, there will sometimes be discrepancies between the purchase order prices and quantities paid versus those expected by suppliers, so some accounts payable staff must be retained to reconcile these issues.

The preceding bullet points reveal that there are a wide array of problems to be overcome before the dramatic improvements of this new process can be realized. However, the enhanced level of automation in the process avoids any possible delays during the closing period within the accounts payable department.

AUTOMATE THREE-WAY MATCHING

The three-way matching process is a manual one at most companies; that is, a clerk matches a supplier invoice to a company purchase order and a receiving document to ensure that the correct quantities (and costs) ordered

are the same ones received and billed. This is a painfully slow and inefficient process, given the large number of documents involved, as well as the
startling number of exceptions that nearly always arise.

There are two ways to solve the problem. One is to dispense with
three-way matching entirely, which requires considerable reengineering of
the accounts payable process, as well as retraining of the receiving staff and
even of suppliers. This process was described in detail in the "Pay Based on
Receiving Approval Only" section earlier in this chapter. Although this is
the most elegant solution, it also requires the most work to implement.

The second solution requires some software changes that may already
be available in the existing software package, with minimal changes to
employee procedures, while still resulting in efficiency improvements
(though not on the scale of the first solution). This concept involves keeping the matching process in its current form but using the computer system
to perform the matching work. In order to automate three-way matching,
all three documents must be entered into the computer system. This is easy
for purchase orders, because most companies already enter them directly
into the computer to track purchase orders through the manufacturing system. The next easiest document to enter is the receiving document, which
can be either a bill of lading or a packing slip. To do so, there should be a
computer terminal at the receiving dock that is linked to the main accounting database so that all information entered at the dock is centrally stored.

Finally, the supplier invoice must be entered into the computer
system—line by line. It is common enough to enter the supplier's invoice
number and total dollar amount into the computer system, but automated
matching requires the complete entry of all line items, quantities, and costs
into the system, which can be a considerable chore. Once this information
is in the accounting database, the computer system automatically matches
the three documents (usually using the purchase order number as the
index), compares all line items, and presents a summary of the matched
documents to the accounting staff, showing any variances between the
matched documents. The accounting staff can then scan the information
and decide if the variances require further analysis or if suppliers can be
paid at once. In short, this concept automates an existing manual procedure without any real procedural enhancements.

REDUCE REQUIRED APPROVALS

The accounts payable process is typically a long one. Part of the problem
is that many accounting systems require a manager's signature (or those of
several managers!) on a supplier invoice before it can be paid. Although it
is reasonable to have such a requirement if there is no purchase order for
the invoice, many systems require the signature even if there is already
a purchase order (which is, in effect, a form of prior approval). Also, most

accounting systems require a manager's signature on unapproved invoices, no matter how small the invoice may be. The result of these common approval procedures is that the accounts payable staff delivers invoices to managers for signatures and then waits until the documents are returned before proceeding further with the payment process. If the manager is not available to sign an invoice, then it sits; if the manager loses the invoice (a common occurrence), the invoice is never paid, resulting in an angry supplier who must send a fresh copy of the invoice for a second pass through the dangerous shoals of the company's approval process. This is a clearly inefficient process, both lengthy and likely to annoy suppliers. What can be done?

A superb improvement concept for any company to implement is to limit approvals to a single event or document and, wherever possible, to limit this approval to a period prior to the receipt of the supplier invoice. For example, an authorized signature on a purchase order should be sufficient overall approval to pay an invoice. After all, if the signature was good enough to authorize the initial purchase of the item or service, shouldn't the same signature be sufficient approval for payment of the supplier's bill? In addition, by shifting the approval to the purchase order, the accounts payable staff does not have to track down someone after the supplier's invoice has been received, which effectively chops time from the overall accounts payable process. Another variation is to use a signature on the purchase requisition, which comes before the purchase order. As long as either document is signed by an authorized person and sent to the accounts payable staff in advance, it does not matter which document is used as authorization. The key is to use a single authorization early in the purchasing process. By making these changes, supplier invoices can be entered into the accounting system more quickly, increasing the odds that their associated expenses will be recognized in the correct accounting period.

One reason why so many companies require multiple approvals—both at the time of purchasing and at the time of payment—is that they do not have a sufficient degree of control over the authorization process. For example, there may not be any real check of authorization signatures when purchase requisitions are converted into purchase orders, nor might there be any required signature when purchase orders are issued to suppliers. In addition, the signature stamp used to sign checks may not be properly controlled. In all of these cases, if there were tight control over the authorization used, there would be a need for only a single authorization. For example, there should be an audit of all purchase orders to ensure that every one of them has been signed, that every signature is by an authorized person, and that the person signing is authorized to purchase what was ordered. This level of control requires continual internal audits to ensure that the control point is working, as well as continual follow-up and training of employees so they know precisely how the control system is supposed to work. Only by instituting this degree of control over authorizations can a company reduce the number of approvals to a minimum.

USE NEGATIVE ASSURANCE FOR INVOICE APPROVALS

One of the largest problems for the accounts payable staff is the continuing delay in receiving approvals of supplier invoices from authorized employees throughout the company. Invoices tend to sit on employee desks as low-priority items, resulting in constant reminders by the accounting staff to turn in documents, which in turn results in late payments and missed early-payment discounts.

This universal problem can be avoided through the use of negative assurance. Under this approval system, invoice copies are sent to authorizing employees and are automatically paid when due unless the employees tell the accounts payable staff *not* to issue payment. By focusing only on those invoices that may be incorrect, the accounting staff can process the vast majority of all submitted invoices without cajoling anyone to submit an approved document.

The process can be streamlined even further by digitizing an incoming invoice and e-mailing it to the authorizing employee. By doing so, employees can be reached even when they are off-site, as long as they check their e-mail regularly. By linking these transmissions to workflow software, the accounting staff can designate how long an invoice can wait in a recipient's e-mail box before it is automatically routed to another authorized person, thereby ensuring that *someone* will see every invoice and raise a red flag if a potential problem exists.

No matter which of these options is used, the result will be faster entry of supplier invoices into the accounting system, so there is less risk of misrepresenting financial results as a result of missing invoices.

USE PROCUREMENT CARDS

Consider the number of work steps required to process a payment to a supplier: receiving paperwork, sorting and matching it, entering data into a computer, routing invoices through the organization for approvals, expediting those invoices having early-payment discounts, creating month-end accruals, setting up files on new suppliers in the computer and the filing system, processing checks, obtaining check signatures, mailing payments, and filing away check copies. Now consider how many purchases are so small that the cost of all these activities exceeds the cost of the purchase. In many instances, one-quarter or more of all payment transactions fall into this category.

The answer to this problem is not to find a more efficient way to process the supplier invoices but to change the way in which these items or services are purchased. Instead of using a purchase order or check to purchase something, one should instead use a procurement card. Also known as a purchasing card, a procurement card is simply a credit card with a few additional features. It is issued to those people making frequent purchases, with instructions to keep on making the same purchases, but to do so with the card. This eliminates many supplier invoices by consolidating them all into a single monthly credit card statement.

Because there is always a risk of having a user purchase extraneous items with a procurement card, including cash advances or excessively expensive items, the card includes a few features to control precisely what is purchased. For example, it can have a limitation on the total daily amount purchased, the total amount purchased per transaction, or the total purchased per month. It may also limit purchases to a specific store or to only those stores falling into a specific Standard Industry Code (SIC) category, such as a plumbing supply store and nothing else. These built-in controls effectively reduce the risk that procurement cards will be misused.

Once the credit card statement arrives, it may be too jumbled, with hundreds of purchases, to determine the expense accounts to which all of the items are to be charged. To help matters, a company can specify how the credit card statement is to be sorted by the credit card processing company; it can list expenses by the location of each purchase, by SIC, or by dollar amount, as well as by date. It is even possible to receive an electronic transmission of the credit card statement so a company can sort its own expenses. The purchasing limitations and expense statement changes are the key differences between a regular credit card and a procurement card.

Another feature provided by those entities offering procurement cards is Level II data; this includes a supplier's minority supplier status, incorporated status, and its tax identification number. Another option to look into when reviewing the procurement card option is the existence of Level III reporting, which includes such line-item details as quantities, product codes, product descriptions, and freight and duty costs—in short, the bulk of the information needed to maintain a detailed knowledge of exactly what is being bought with a company's procurement cards. Most major national suppliers of credit cards can supply Level II or Level III data.

The American Express Corporate Card has now expanded the range of uses to which its procurement card can be put by allowing for the inclusion of many recurring business expenses, such as long-distance phone bills, Internet services, monthly parking, wireless phone bills, and office security systems. By having suppliers send their bills to American Express, the accounts payable staff can consolidate the quantity of check payments that it must make to just a single credit card payment. American Express also provides a Summary of Account that itemizes all of the business expenses for which payments are being made, which provides sufficient proof for account auditing purposes.

There are two ways to set up invoices to run through this procurement card. The first approach is to refer to American Express's list of existing companies that are willing to provide this service. Second, if the company wants to add a supplier to this list, it can contact American Express, which will call the supplier to request a rebilling to it. One issue with this service is that the company must notify its suppliers if its American Express card number changes, because they will continue to send their billings to the old number unless otherwise notified. Also, it may take several months to line up a sufficient number of suppliers to see a significant reduction in the number of checks issued by the accounts payable department.

Although this best practice may appear to be nirvana to many organizations, the following issues must be carefully considered to ensure that the program operates properly:

- *Card misuse.* When procurement cards are handed out to a large number of employees, there is always the risk that someone will abuse the privilege and use valuable company funds on incorrect or excessive purchases. There are several ways to either prevent this problem or reduce its impact. One approach is to hand out the procurement cards only to the purchasing staff, who can use them to pay for items for which they would otherwise issue a purchase order; however, this does not address the large quantity of very small purchases that other employees may make, so a better approach is a gradual rollout of procurement cards to those employees who have shown a continuing pattern of making small purchases. Also, the characteristics of the procurement card can be altered, by limiting the dollar amount of purchases either per transaction, per time period, or even per department. One can also restrict the number of usages per day. An additional method for avoiding employee misuse of procurement cards is to have them sign an agreement describing the sanctions that will be imposed if the cards are misused, which may include termination. Some mix of these solutions can mitigate the risk of procurement card abuse.

- *Spending on special items.* The use of a procurement card can actually interfere with existing internal procedures for the purchase of some special items, rendering those systems less efficient. For example, an automated materials planning system for the inventory can issue purchase orders to suppliers with no manual intervention; adding inventory items to this situation that were purchased through a different methodology can interfere with the integrity of the database, requiring more manual reconciliation of inventory quantities. Thus, procurement cards are not always a good idea when buying inventory items. Also, capital purchases typically have to go through a detailed review and approval process before they are acquired; because a procurement card offers an easy way to buy smaller capital items, it represents a simple way to bypass the approval process. Thus, they are not a good choice for capital purchases.

- *Dealing with users of the old system.* Some employees will not take to the new procurement card approach, if only because they are used to the old system. This can cause headaches for both the purchasing and accounting departments, because they must deal with both the old system and the new one in combination. It may be impossible to completely eliminate the old purchase order system in some cases (if only because of company politics), so a good alternative is to charge to those departments using the old system the fully burdened cost of each transaction that does not use a procurement card. Because this burdened cost, which includes the cost of all the processing steps noted at the beginning of this section, can easily exceed $100 per transaction, it becomes an effective way to shift usage toward the procurement card solution.

- *Summarizing general ledger accounts.* The summary statements that are received from the credit card processor will not contain as many expense line items as are probably already contained within a company's general ledger (which tends to divide expenses into many categories). For example, the card statements may categorize only by shop supplies, office supplies, and shipping supplies. If so, then it is best to alter the general ledger accounts to match the categories being reported through the procurement cards. This may also require changes to the budgeting system, which probably mirrors the accounts used in the general ledger.

- *Purchases from unapproved suppliers.* A company may have negotiated favorable prices from a few select suppliers in exchange for making all of its purchases for certain items from them. It is a simple matter to ensure that purchases are made through these suppliers when the purchasing department is placed in direct control of the buying process. However, once purchases are put in the hands of anyone with a procurement card, it is much less likely that the same level of discipline will occur. Instead, purchases will be made from a much larger group of suppliers. Although not an easy issue to control, the holders of procurement cards can at least be issued a "preferred supplier yellow pages," which lists those suppliers from whom they should be buying. Their adherence to this list can be tracked by comparing actual purchases to the yellow pages list and giving them feedback about the issue.

- *Paying sales and use taxes.* Occasionally, a state sales tax auditor will arrive on a company's doorstep, demanding to see documentation that proves it has paid a sales tax on all items purchased. This is not easy to do when procurement cards are used, not only because there may be a multitude of poorly organized supplier receipts, but also because the sales tax noted on a credit card payment slip shows only the grand total sales tax paid, rather than the sales tax for each item purchased; this is an important issue, because some items are exempt from taxation, which will result in a total sales tax that appears to be too low in comparison to the total dollar amount of items purchased.

One way to alleviate this problem is to obtain sales tax exemption certificates from all states in which a company does business; employees then present the sales tax exemption number whenever they make purchases, so that there is no doubt at all—no sales taxes have been paid. Then the accounting staff can calculate the grand total for the use tax (which is the same thing as the sales tax, except that the purchaser pays it to the state, rather than to the seller) to pay, and forward this to the appropriate taxing authority. An alternative is to "double bag" tax payments, which means that the company pays the full use tax on all procurement card purchases, without bothering to spend the time figuring out what sales taxes have already been paid. This is a safe approach from a tax audit perspective and may not involve much additional cost if the total of all procurement card purchases is small. Yet another alternative is the reverse—to ignore the entire sales tax issue and confront only it when audited; this decision is usually based on the controller's level of risk tolerance.

Although the problems noted here must be addressed, one must understand the significance of the advantages of using procurement cards in order to see why the problems are minor in relation to the possible benefits. The main attractions of this improvement concept are:

- *Fewer accounting transactions.* Some of the accounts payable staff may be redirected to other tasks, because the number of transactions will drop considerably.

- *Fewer invoice reviews and signatures.* Managers no longer have to review a considerable number of invoices for payment approval, nor do they have to sign so many checks addressed to suppliers.

- *No cash advances.* Whenever an employee asks for a cash advance, the accounting staff must create a manual check for that person, record it in the accounting records, and ensure that it is paid back by the employee. This can be a time-consuming process in proportion to the generally meager advances given to employees. A credit card can avoid this entire process, because employees can go to an automated teller machine and withdraw cash, which will appear in the next monthly card statement from the issuing bank—no check issuances required. This benefit applies only if those employees needing cash advances are the same ones with access to a procurement card.

- *Fewer petty cash transactions.* If employees have procurement cards, they will no longer feel compelled to buy items with their own cash and then ask for a reimbursement from the company's petty cash fund.

- *Fewer purchasing transactions.* A whole range of purchasing activities are reduced in volume, including contacting suppliers for quotes, creating and mailing purchase orders, resolving invoicing differences, and closing out orders.

- *Reduced supplier list.* The number of active vendors in the purchasing database can be greatly reduced, which allows the buying staff to focus on better relations with the remaining ones on the list.

- *Reduced mail room volume.* Even the mail room will experience a drop in volume, because there will be far fewer incoming supplier invoices and outgoing company checks.

It is apparent that the use of procurement cards does not directly affect the closing process, although it will reduce the total volume of payables transactions. This can yield more available time by the payables staff to work on other department projects, which may include closing-related activities.

A procurement card is easy to implement, but one should keep a significant difficulty in mind: The banks that issue credit cards must expend extra labor to set up a procurement card for a company, because each one must be custom designed. Consequently, they prefer to issue procurement cards only to those companies that can show a significant volume of credit card business—usually at least $1 million per year. This volume limitation makes it difficult for a smaller company to use procurement cards. The problem can be partially avoided by using a group of supplier-specific credit cards. For example, a company can sign up for a credit card with its office supply store, another with its building materials store, and yet another with its electrical supplies store. This results in a somewhat larger number of credit card statements per month, but they are already sorted by supplier, so they are essentially a poor man's procurement card.

HAVE SUPPLIERS INCLUDE THEIR SUPPLIER NUMBERS ON INVOICES

The typical vendor database includes listings for thousands of suppliers. Every time an invoice arrives from a supplier, the accounts payable staff must scroll through the list to determine the vendor code for each one. If there are similar names for different suppliers, or multiple locations for the same one, it is likely that the resulting check payments will go astray, leading to lots of extra time to sort through who should have been paid. This basic problem can be partially resolved by having suppliers include the supplier number, as created by the company's accounting system, on their invoices. The easiest way to do so is to mail out a change-of-address form to all suppliers, listing the same company address, but also noting as part of the address an "accounts payable code" that includes the supplier number. Suppliers will gladly add this line to the mailing address to which they send their invoices, because they think a routing code will expedite payment to them (which, in a way, it will). Some follow-up may be necessary to ensure that all suppliers adopt this extra address line. Even if not all of the suppliers elect to make the change, there will still be an increase in efficiency caused by those that have done so.

There are two problems with this approach. One is that the change of address mailing cannot be a bulk mailing of the same letter, because each letter must include the supplier code that is unique to each recipient. This will call for a mail merge software application that can create a unique letter for each recipient. The other problem is that new suppliers (i.e., those arriving *after* the bulk mailing) must be given a supplier code at the time they are first set up on the system. This may require a special phone call to the supplier's accounts payable department to ensure that the code is added to their address file or a periodic mailing to all new suppliers that specifies their supplier codes.

RECEIVE BILLINGS THROUGH ELECTRONIC DATA INTERCHANGE

Many of the larger companies, especially those in the retailing industry, have been using electronic data interchange (EDI) for some time. This section describes what EDI is, how it works, why more companies should use it, and why so many do not.

EDI involves the transfer of electronic documents between companies. These documents are sent in strictly defined formats, of which there are over a hundred, one for each type of standard company transaction, including a supplier billing. These formats tend to be large and complex because they are designed for use by multiple industries; most companies need to fill out only a small portion of each EDI message. Once completed, an EDI message is transmitted to the recipient. This can be done directly, but it usually goes to a third-party provider that maintains a mainframe computer that receives messages from many subscribing companies. The message recipient dials into its electronic mailbox at the third-party's mainframe (usually several times a day) to pick up any EDI messages. The recipient then enters each EDI message into its own system for further processing. The reader may notice that a company could achieve the same rapid transfer of information by sending a fax with the same information. This is true, but if properly installed, EDI allows for a greater degree of automation by linking directly into a company's computer system. For example, a paper-based fax must be rekeyed into the recipient's computer system, whereas an EDI message is in a standardized electronic format and so can be run through an automatic conversion program that enters data into the recipient's computer system with no manual data entry work at all. The feature gives EDI a distinct advantage over a fax transmission.

Larger companies use EDI most frequently because it allows them to automatically process large quantities of transactions with no manual data entry work, which can be important when hundreds or thousands of transactions are flowing through the system. When data is entered by hand, there is a potential for errors in the keypunching, which probably means that there will be an inordinate number of manmade errors to correct in these larger companies, given the volumes of data that must be entered. Thus, EDI allows them to avoid not only the expense of data entry but also the expense of tracking down and fixing data entry errors.

If EDI makes a company so efficient, why are only the largest companies using it? The answer is simple: It is expensive to implement and only the largest transaction volumes will offset the cost of the initial setup. For example, if a company wants to receive all of its accounts payable billings by EDI, it must first contact each supplier and persuade it to send EDI transmissions, set up procedures between the two companies for doing so, and then test the system before going live. In addition, the true labor savings will be realized only if the incoming EDI messages are automatically entered into the recipient's computer system, which calls for the customized programming of an automated interface between the EDI system and the recipient's computer system; this can be an expensive undertaking. Most suppliers will not want to participate in this system unless there are significant transaction volumes between them and the company—why go to the trouble for a small customer? In short, EDI is not catching on in smaller companies because of the expense and effort of installing the system, plus the difficulty of forcing suppliers to participate. Although larger companies may convince their direct trading partners to use EDI, this concept will spread through the ranks of smaller companies only with the greatest difficulty.

Despite the difficulties enumerated here, a fully automated EDI system is an excellent avenue for receiving supplier invoices without delays caused by postal float or manual data entry. This has a favorable impact on the speed with which supplier invoices can be recorded at month-end.

REQUEST THAT SUPPLIERS ENTER INVOICES THROUGH A WEB SITE

A company may be experiencing some difficulty in persuading its suppliers to switch over to the transmission of invoices by EDI, which would allow it to automatically process all incoming invoices without any data rekeying. A typical complaint when this request is made is that special EDI software must be purchased and stored in a separate computer, while someone must be trained, not only in how to use the software, but also in how to reformat the invoicing data into the format used by the EDI transaction. This problem can be partially avoided by having suppliers access a Web site where they can conduct the data entry.

By having suppliers enter data into a Web site instead of through an EDI transaction, they can avoid the need for any special software that is stored on an in-house computer. A Web site merely requires Internet access, which is commonly available through most computers. Once the data has been entered at the Web site, a company can shift the data into an automated EDI transaction processing program that will convert the data into an EDI format and transmit it to the company's accounting system. Thus, suppliers can use either EDI or Web-based data entry to send invoices to a company, which will process them both in EDI format.

There are some costs associated with this concept. One is that the company may have to use special discounts or early payments to convince suppliers to use the Web site, rather than mailing in their invoices. Also, the Web site must be constructed and maintained, while other software must be created that converts the incoming transactions into EDI format and then ports the resulting data to the accounting system for further processing. Consequently, this can be a relatively expensive option to implement, and so may be useful only for those organizations experiencing a large volume of transactions.

From the perspective of the closing process, this is a less favorable approach than a fully automated EDI system, because it may take several days for some suppliers to manually enter invoices through a company Web site.

AUDIT EXPENSE REPORTS

A labor-intensive task for the accounts payable employees involves carefully reviewing every line item on employee expense reports, comparing everything to the company policy for allowable travel or entertainment expenses, and then contacting employees regarding inconsistencies prior to issuing a check. For a larger company with many traveling employees, this can be an extraordinarily labor-intensive task. Furthermore, most employees create accurate expense reports, so the labor expended by the accounts payable staff is rarely equal to the cost savings all the review work generates. To make the situation more unbearable for employees, the expense reviews take so long to complete that there can be a serious delay before an employee receives payment for a check, especially if the expense report is rejected because of reporting failures by the employee, resulting in the expense report moving back and forth several times between the employee and the accounting department before it is paid. When there is so much document travel time, it is also common for the expense report to be "lost in the shuffle," meaning that the employee may have to recreate the expense report and resubmit it. All of these factors result in an inefficient process in the accounting department and lots of angry employees who are waiting for reimbursement. Furthermore, expense reports may be so delayed that they are recorded in a later accounting period, which impacts the accuracy of the financial statements.

The solution is to replace a total review of all expense reports with an occasional audit. This approach involves taking a sample of many employees' expense reports every few months and comparing the reported results to the company travel and entertainment policy to see if there are any exceptions. If the exceptions are significant, it may be necessary to follow up with additional reviews of the expense reports of the same employees to investigate possible abuse. The audit usually results in a list of common expense reporting problems, as well as the names of employees who are abusing the expense reporting system. There are several solutions to ongoing expense reporting problems:

- *Employee education.* It may be necessary to periodically reissue the company policy on travel and entertainment, with follow-up calls to specific abusers to reinforce the policy. This advance work keeps problems from showing up on expense reports.

- *Flag employees for continual audits.* If some employees simply cannot create a correct expense report, they can be scheduled for ongoing audits to ensure that every report they create is reviewed for accuracy.

- *Flag employees for complete reviews by the accounts payable staff.* Some employees may be so inept at issuing proper expense reports that their reports must be totally reviewed prior to reimbursement. These problem employees can be flagged during the audits.

The audit work is usually carried out by the internal audit department, rather than the accounts payable personnel, because the internal auditors are appropriately experienced in such review work.

When using this concept, there can be a concern that employee reporting abuses will go unnoticed until an auditor finds a problem after the fact. This is a legitimate concern. However, when the audit staff selects expenses, reports for review, they should stratify the sample of reports so there is a preponderance of expensive expense reports in the sample, which means that any potentially exorbitant abuses will have a greater chance of being discovered. Although these discoveries will be after the fact, when employees have already been paid, the company can still seek reimbursement, especially if the employees are still on the payroll, so that adjustments can be taken from their paychecks. However, if employees have already left the company, any overpayments probably cannot be reimbursed.

In short, replacing a total review of all expense reports with an occasional audit can significantly reduce the workload of the accounts payable staff, although there is some risk that employee reporting abuses will result in large overpayments prior to discovery.

AUTOMATE EXPENSE REPORTING

One of the tasks of the accounts payable staff is to check carefully all of the expenses reported in an employee's expense report to ensure that all expenses are valid and have the correct supporting documentation. This can be a major task if there are many expense reports. This will be the case if a company is large or has a large proportion of personnel who travel, which is common if a company is in the consulting or sales fields. Luckily, some companies have found a way to get around all of this review work.

An improvement concept that nearly eliminates the expense report review work of the accounts payable staff is to create a "smart" computer program that walks an employee through the expense reporting process, flagging problem expenses as soon as they are entered and requiring backup receipts for only selected items. The system is highly customized, because the review rules will vary by company. For example, one company may have a policy of requiring backup receipts for all meals, whereas another company may automatically hand out a per-diem meals payment and will not care about meal receipts. Such variations in expense reporting policies will inevitably result in an automated expense reporting system that is closely tailored to each company's needs; such a system should probably be programmed in-house, which is an expensive undertaking. Because of the high level of expense, this concept will pay for itself only if it offsets a great deal of accounts payable work, so there should be a very large number of expense reports being submitted before anyone tries to implement the concept.

The logical flow of automated expense reporting is noted in the following processing steps:

1. The user accesses an online expense reporting form that is linked to the central expense reporting software and database.

2. The user enters expenses by date and category.

3. The software reviews all expenses as entered and flags those that are not allowable. It rejects these and notifies the user, along with an explanation.

4. The software reviews all remaining expenses and decides which items require a backup receipt.

5. The user prints out a transmittal form detailing all required receipts and also containing a unique transmittal number linked to the expense report just entered into the computer system.

6. Upon completion by the user, the electronic expense report is routed by e-mail to the user's supervisor, who electronically approves or rejects the report. If rejected, the supervisor can note the problem

on the expense report, which is then routed back to the user for resubmission.

7. The user attaches all receipts to the transmittal form and mails it to the accounts payable department.

8. When the accounts payable department receives the transmittal form and receipts, it verifies that all receipts are included and that the expense report has been approved by the supervisor, and then approves the entire package.

9. Upon approval by the accounts payable staff, the expense report is immediately paid by wire transfer to the bank account of the user.

10. The transmittal form and receipts are filed.

Although there appear to be more steps in the automated process than in the traditional one, the extra steps are automatic or much simpler. The overall result is far less manual processing time, as well as a significant reduction in the time needed before an employee is paid.

The solution just noted is for an automated employee expense reporting system that is entirely custom programmed. However, many organizations do not process a sufficient number of employee expense reports to justify the cost of all the programming time required to create the system. For these companies, a good alternative is to purchase an automated expense reporting software package. These packages are entirely self-contained and do an effective job of processing employee expense reports, but they do not provide direct linkages to the rest of a company's accounting system. For this linkage, a custom-designed interface module is still required. A Web-based expense reporting package is especially useful, because employees in outlying locations or who are traveling can use the system at any location where they can access the Internet; moreover, this system requires no software installation on anyone's computer. Also, Web-based software can be updated easily, whereas client-server systems require updates on individual user computers. Furthermore, if someone steals an employee's computer, there will be no time or expense information stored on it, because this information is submitted directly through the Internet to a different storage location. Examples of such packages are made by Concur Technologies, GEAC Extensity, IBM, Oracle, and SAP.

LINK CORPORATE TRAVEL POLICIES TO AN AUTOMATED EXPENSE REPORTING SYSTEM

The typical set of travel policies used by a company is quite detailed: *Thou shalt not charge to the company the cost of movies, clothing, first-class upgrades, and so on.* However, the overburdened accounts payable staff has little time to review expense reports for these items, much less to then create variance reports and send them out to the violating employees and their supervisors. An additional problem is that corporate travel policies change with some regularity, which makes it difficult for the accounts payable staff to even know which policies are still valid. A further problem arises when a company reimburses its employees based on the per-diem rates listed in the Federal Travel Regulation. This document is used by the federal government to determine a reasonable cost of living at each of more than 100 cities throughout the country; given the frequency of change in these numbers (at least quarterly), it becomes labor intensive to determine what payments to make to employees. However, these problems can be eliminated by converting the travel policies into rules that can be used by a computer to automatically spot problems with expense reports that have been submitted through an automated expense reporting system.

For example, input from a corporate travel card into an automated expense reporting system can tell if an airfare is for a first-class seat, which may be prohibited by company travel policy. If the first-class purchase can be set up as a flagged field, then the computer system can automatically spot this issue and either note it on a report or (more proactively) send an e-mail to the appropriate person that notes the issue. Examples of other rules violations are to verify that the correct airline was used (because there may be a bulk-purchase agreement in place) and that restaurant bills were actually incurred during the period spanned by a business trip (rather than before or after, which would be suspicious). However, this sort of early-warning system can be expensive to create. There are no standard software packages that perform this task, so the programming staff must be called on to convert policies into rules that can be understood by the computer system, and then set up an interface between the rules database and the expense report database that will spot rule violations. In short, this can be an expensive option to install, and so should be considered only if there is a clear likelihood that there will be significant resulting cost savings.

ISSUE A STANDARD ACCOUNT CODE LIST

Accounts payable can be a difficult area in which to replace employees while still experiencing high levels of productivity. The problem is caused by the time it takes a new person to learn the accounts to which invoices should be coded. When experienced accounts payable clerks are hired, they still must memorize the account codes, which will slow them down considerably. Even an experienced, long-term employee may occasionally misdirect a supplier invoice to the wrong account.

The easiest solution is to reduce the chart of accounts down to a single page of key accounts to which invoices are to be coded. Most invoices can be applied to a very small number of accounts, so this is usually a viable option. When the shortened list is posted at each accounts payable clerk's desk, it becomes a simple reference tool for finding the correct account, which improves productivity while reducing the error rate.

A more sophisticated way to resolve the problem is to encode the accounting software with an account number for each supplier. Under this method, the clerk does not have to worry about the account to which anything should be coded because the computer already contains the information. However, there are two problems with this approach: (1) Some basic software packages do not contain this feature; and (2) the default account code may not match the nature of the specific invoice line item for which the supplier is billing. Given the trend toward supplier consolidation, it is increasingly likely that a company will use one supplier for a wide range of products and services, so several account codes may apply to a single supplier, rendering a default account code useless.

LINK SUPPLIER REQUESTS TO THE ACCOUNTS PAYABLE DATABASE

A significant task for an accounts payable person, especially one working for a company that pays its bills late, is to answer payment queries from suppliers. They want to know when their invoices were paid, the amount of the payments, and the check numbers that were issued. For a company that is seriously delinquent in its payments, this can be a full-time job for the accounting staff, which is also a clear loss of productive time. It is a particularly vexing issue during the core closing period, when the accounting staff has no time to field questions from suppliers.

A recent innovation that largely eliminates verbal responses to suppliers is to have them call a phone number linking them to a keypad-activated inquiry system that answers their most common questions. For example, they can enter the company's purchase order number, their invoice number, or the supplier's name; the system will then respond with the specific payments made, the date on which the check was cut, and the check number. The system can even be extended to list the date on which payments are scheduled to be made.

However, there are some issues to consider before installing an automated supplier response system. One problem is that this is a recent innovation, and so most suppliers will not be used to it—they want to talk to a person and will deluge the company's operator to voice this opinion. To quell this type of response, the system should include an option to exit the automated system and contact a person. This allows the more technologically versed suppliers to use the automated system, whereas other users can still talk to a person. This option is also necessary for those cases where there are unusual circumstances. For example, a company may not be paying because of a lack of receiving documentation or because the quantity billed was incorrect; it is better to discuss these problems with a person instead of a computer, because special actions may need to be taken to resolve the situation.

The other problem is the cost of the installation. It requires an interface computer linked to the main accounting system, as well as modem access and software to translate supplier requests into inquiries that the accounting database can answer. These costs can be considerable, especially when there are expected to be many callers and therefore many requests for information. The price range typically starts at $20,000 for the smallest installations and can be many times higher for large ones. Nonetheless, this is a good approach for companies that believe they can bring about a major efficiency improvement by routing suppliers straight to the accounts payable database for information.

An alternative to having suppliers access accounts payable information through a phone connection is to do so through an Internet site. This approach is somewhat more flexible than a voice-activated system that is generally limited to a few simple status messages. Instead, a Web page can itemize the exact status of each payable item, assign a code to it that explains the reasons for any delays, and note the name of the contact person in the accounts payable department who is responsible for processing the supplier invoice. It can also list any missing information that is delaying payment, such as a purchase order number or bank account number for the supplier, which can be entered by the supplier directly into the Web site and which will be automatically loaded into the accounting database to assist in payment processing. The Web page may even list the name of the person who is responsible for approving the invoice, as well as this person's contact information.

AUTOMATE PAYMENTS FOR REPETITIVE PROCESSING

The typical company has a small proportion of invoices that arrive at regular intervals and are for the same amount, month after month. Examples of such payments are rent invoices or lease payments. These payments usually go through the standard accounts payable matching process, including searches for approval documents, before they are paid. However, it is possible to utilize their repetitive nature to create a more efficient subprocess within the accounts payable area.

The concept that streamlines repetitive supplier invoices is to create a payment schedule to bypass the approval process and automatically issue a check in a prespecified amount and on a prespecified date. This can be done by creating a table of repetitive payments in the accounting computer system, but there is no reason why the programming expense cannot be avoided by listing the payments on a piece of paper and posting it in the accounts payable area. In either case, there is no need to look for approvals, so there is less labor required of the accounts payable staff. However, there are two problems. First, the repetitive payment schedule must note the termination date of each payment, so that checks are not inadvertently issued after the final payment date. These payments can be time consuming when the supplier returns them. Second, the repetitive payments may change from time to time, so the schedule must note both the dates when payment amounts change and the amounts of the changes. For example, rental payments frequently contain preset escalation clauses, which must be recognized by the repetitive payment schedule.

An especially fine use for repetitive invoicing is the remittance of garnishments to various courts on behalf of employees. In the case of child support payments, these garnishments may go on for years and usually in the same amount throughout the entire period (unless the court orders that a different amount be withheld from time to time). Repetitive invoicing is useful here, because a company is liable to the court to make these payments and can be subject to onerous penalties if it does not do so. By shifting the burden of making this payment to the computer system, there is less risk of not making the payment.

Automating repetitive payments that occur in the same amounts and on the same dates is a good way to remove the approval step from the accounts payable process, although this improvement typically covers only a small percentage of the total workload of the accounts payable staff.

ELIMINATE MANUAL CHECKS

The accounts payable process can be streamlined through the use of many improvement concepts that are listed in this chapter; however, a common recurring problem is those payments that go around the entire preplanned payable process. These are the inevitable payments that are sudden and unplanned and that must be handled immediately. Examples are payments for pizza deliveries, flowers for bereaved employees, or cash-on-delivery payments. In all of these cases, the accounting staff must drop what it is doing, create a manual check, get it signed, and enter the information on the check into the computer system. To make matters worse, because of the rush basis of the payment, it is common for the accounting person to forget to enter the transaction into the accounting database, which in turn throws off the bank reconciliation during the month-end closing process, which creates still more work to track down and fix the problem. In short, issuing manual checks significantly worsens the efficiency of the accounts payable staff.

One can use three methods to reduce the number of manual checks. The first method is to cut off the inflow of check requests, while the second is (paradoxically) to automate the cutting of manual checks. The first approach is difficult, because it requires tallying the manual checks that were cut each month and following up with the check requesters to see if there might be a more orderly manner of making requests in the future, thereby allowing more checks to be issued through the normal accounts payable process. Unfortunately, this practice requires so much time communicating with the check requesters that the lost time will overtake the resulting time savings by the accounting staff caused by writing fewer manual checks. The second approach is to preset a printer with check stock, so that anyone can request a check at any time, and an accounting person can immediately sit down at a computer terminal, enter the check information, and have it print out at once. This approach has the unique benefit of avoiding any trouble with not reentering information into the computer system, because it is being entered there in the first place (which avoids any future problems with the bank reconciliation). It tends to take slightly longer to create a check in this manner, but the overall time savings are greater. If one adopts this approach, remember to offset the cost of the printer against the likely time savings from creating a more rapid response to manual check requests.

A third alternative is to make the process of creating a manual check so difficult that requesters will avoid it. For example, the request may require the signature of a senior manager (who will be less than happy to be interrupted for a signature) or multiple approving signatures. In addition, the accounting department could charge an exorbitant amount for this service to the requesting department. Furthermore, a report itemizing all manual check requests can be sent to senior management each month, highlighting who is bothering the accounting staff with these items.

Any combination of these actions should reduce the use of manual checks or at least enhance the efficiency with which they are processed.

USE A SIGNATURE STAMP

One of the most common delay points in the accounts payable process is when an accounting clerk must go in search of someone to sign checks. If only one person is so authorized and not always available, it can keep any checks from being issued at all. The situation grows worse when multiple signatures are required for multiple checks. On top of these delays, it is also common for the check signers to require backup documents for each check being signed, which requires a considerable extra effort by the accounting staff, not only to clip the correct documents to each check, but also to unclip the documents after the checks are signed and file them away in the appropriate files (which also increases the risk that the documents will be filed in the wrong place). This is an exceptional waste of time, because it does not add a whit of value to the process.

The solution to this multitude of inefficiencies is to eliminate check signing completely. Instead of assuming that there must be a complete review of all checks prior to signing, one must get management used to the idea of installing approvals earlier in the process, thus eliminating approval at the point of check signing. Once management is comfortable with this idea, one must still comply with bank regulations, which require a signature on each check; this is now a matter of finding the easiest way to stamp checks, rather than following a rigid approval process. Check stamping can be accomplished most simply by creating a signature stamp from the signature of an authorized check signer, which then requires that someone stamp all checks by hand. A more efficient approach is to digitize an authorized signature and incorporate it into the check-printing program, so the signature is automatically affixed to each check with no manual intervention.

The only problem with a signature stamp is that it can be misused to sign unauthorized checks or legal documents. This problem can be avoided by locking up the signature stamp in the company safe and severely limiting access to the safe. It may also be necessary to separately lock up check stock, thereby making it doubly difficult for anyone to issue an unauthorized signed check.

By using a signature stamp, one can eliminate the time wasted to find a check signer, while also avoiding the work required to attach backup documents to checks and then file these documents subsequent to review.

IGNORE SUPPLIER INVOICES AND PAY FROM STATEMENTS

Many suppliers provide frequent deliveries and services, each one for small amounts of money. They tend to send large volumes of invoices, which can inundate the accounts payable staff. Also, given the high volume of invoices received, it is possible that some invoices will be mistakenly paid twice, especially if there are no invoice numbers that the computer system can check for duplicate payments.

One solution to these high-volume, low-cost invoices is to throw them all away. Then, when the suppliers send the usual month-end statement of invoices outstanding, just record the statement in the computer system, using the statement date as the invoice number, and issue a single payment from that document. This also works well for the supplier, who receives just one check instead of many. The only problem with this approach is if the underlying invoices would normally be charged to different departments, which would require one to see the content of those invoices. However, in most cases these invoices are so small that an incorrect or missing expense allocation would have little impact on departmental financial statements. In order to ensure that these statements are received in time for the month-end close, arrange to have suppliers create the statements a few days prior to month-end and fax them to the accounts payable department to avoid any delays caused by the postal service.

ISSUE STANDARD ADJUSTMENT LETTERS TO SUPPLIERS

When the accounts payable staff has a valid reason for making a deduction from a payment to a supplier, this can result in a prolonged series of complaints from the supplier, who is wondering why a short payment was made. The adjustment will appear on the next monthly statement of unpaid invoices from the supplier and will likely end with a series of irate collection calls. If supplier contacts intrude on the core closing period, this can cause significant closing delays. At some point, the accounting staff may feel that the cost savings from taking the deduction was not worth the effort required to convince the supplier of the reasoning behind it.

This issue can be solved to some extent by checking off a box on a standard adjustment letter and mailing the letter to the supplier. The letter should note the invoice number at issue, as well as a series of common problems that caused the short payment to be made. The accounting staff can quickly check off the appropriate box and mail it out, using far less time than would be required to construct a formal, customized letter of notification. The letter should contain space for a free-form written description of the issue, in case it is a unique one not covered by any of the standard explanations already listed on the letter.

SUMMARY

This chapter covered ways to improve the efficiency of the accounts payable function. Although these changes will not have a demonstrably significant impact on the closing process, they can be used to squeeze a small amount of time from the close. As the duration of the closing process begins to approach one day, it becomes increasingly difficult to shave more time from the closing process; at this point the efficiency changes noted here will allow for modest additional time reductions.

ENDNOTE

1. Some sections of this chapter were adapted with permission from Chapter 3 of Bragg, *Accounting Best Practices*, 5th Edition (Hoboken, NJ: John Wiley & Sons, Inc., 2007).

12

Closing the Cash Processing Function[1]

The past few chapters have addressed efficiency improvements in all of the functional areas involved in the closing process. This chapter concludes the efficiency review by addressing improvements to the cash processing function. As was the case in Chapter 11, none of the changes noted here will result in massive improvements to the speed of the close. Nonetheless, they will result in small incremental changes that can shave some time off the duration of the close.

ACCESS BANK ACCOUNT INFORMATION ON THE INTERNET

If the accounting staff needs to know the current balance outstanding on a loan, savings, or checking account balance, the most common way to find out is to call the company's bank representative. This is a slow and sometimes inaccurate approach, because the representative may not be available or may misread the information appearing on the screen. More progressive companies have purchased software from their banks that allows them to dial into the bank database to view this information directly. Although this approach is reasonable, a cost is associated with the modem and software, and a time delay occurs while the modem connects to the bank's database. Also, much of this software is relatively primitive and is character-based, rather than graphics-based.

An easier approach is to provide bank customers with direct access to their account information through a Web site. This access is usually free, requires no special software besides an Internet browser, and can be accessed at once, if the user is connected to a direct-access Internet connection, such as a digital subscriber line (DSL), cable modem, or T1 phone line. The better Web sites are also heavily engineered to be easy-to-read, with online, automated help text to walk the user through the screens. This is becoming such a powerful tool that users should consider switching their bank accounts to those financial institutions that offer this service. It is a particularly effective tool for removing the bank reconciliation from the core closing period, because one can easily use online information to conduct a daily bank reconciliation. By doing so, all unrecorded transactions, banking errors, and bank fees can be investigated and recorded throughout the month, leaving no reconciliation work to handle during the core closing period.

AVOID DELAYS IN CHECK POSTING

When there is a sudden influx of checks, the accounting staff may require an extra day to post them all against the accounts receivable database. This delay can also occur when the payments being made are slightly different from the invoices they are paying, which requires some delay while the differences are reconciled. Although these problems can create a real bottleneck in the accounting department, they also result in a lengthening of the time interval before the checks are deposited at the bank, which in turn results in lost investment income. This can also result in an incorrectly low cash balance at month-end, which may violate a company's loan covenants.

To avoid this problem, the accounting staff can photocopy checks as they arrive, so that postings can be done from the copies, rather than the original checks. This allows the deposit to be made at once, rather than waiting. The main problem with this approach is the danger that a check will not be copied, or that the copy will be lost, which results in a missing posting to the accounts receivable database. This problem leads to downstream collections and research problems involving backtracking to find the missing checks. This problem can be avoided through proper reconciliation procedures that match the total number of copied checks to the total number of actual checks, as well as the total amount posted to the total amount on the copied checks.

This technique can be used in a more deliberate fashion as part of the core closing period. If the accounting staff has no time during the month-end closing to post payments in the accounting system, it can make copies of all checks, deposit the originals, and wait until the close has been completed before using the copies to post payments.

COLLECT RECEIVABLES THROUGH LOCKBOXES

Several problems are associated with receiving all customer payments at a company location. For example, checks can be lost or delayed in the mail room, given to the wrong accounting person for further processing, or delayed in transit from the company to the bank. It is also necessary for the mail room staff to log in all received checks, which are later compared to the deposit slip sent out by the accounting staff to ensure that all received checks have been deposited—this is a non-value-added step, although it is necessary to provide some control over received checks. All of these steps are needed if checks are received and processed directly by a company.

The answer is to have a bank receive the checks instead. To do so, a company's bank sets up a lockbox, which is essentially a separate mailbox to which deposits are sent by customers. The bank opens all mail arriving at the lockbox, deposits all checks at once, copies the checks, and forwards all check copies and anything else contained in customer remittances to the company. This approach has the advantage of accelerating the flow of cash into a company's bank account, because the lockbox system typically reduces the mail float customers enjoy by at least a day, while also eliminating all of the transaction processing time that a company would also need during its internal cash processing steps. The system can be enhanced further by creating lockboxes at several locations throughout the country, with locations sited close to one's largest customers. Customers then send their funds to the nearest lockbox, which further reduces the mail float and increases the speed with which funds arrive in a company's coffers. If there are multiple lockboxes, one should periodically compare the locations of its lockboxes to those of its customers to ensure that the constantly changing mix of customers does not call for an alteration in the locations of some lockboxes to bring the overall mail-float time down to the lowest possible level.

There are a few problems with lockboxes. First, a bank will charge both a fixed and variable-rate fee for the use of a lockbox. There is a small, fixed monthly fee for the lockbox, plus a charge of a few cents for every processed check. For a company with a very small number of incoming checks, these costs may make it uneconomical to maintain a lockbox. Also, the work required to convince customers to change the company's pay-to address can be considerable. Every customer must be contacted, usually by mail, to inform them of the new lockbox address to which they must now send their payments. If they do not comply (a common occurrence), someone must make a reminder call. If there are many customers, this can be a major task to complete and may not be worthwhile if the sales to each customer are extremely small, because the cost of contacting them may exceed the profit from annual sales to them. Thus, a company with a small number of customers or many low-volume customers may not find it cost effective to use a lockbox.

An additional issue is the number of lockboxes that should be used. A company cannot maintain an infinite number of them, because each one has a fixed cost that can add up. Instead, a common approach is to periodically hire a consultant, sometimes provided by a bank, who analyzes the locations and average sales to all customers, calculates the average mail float for each one, and offsets this information with the cost of putting lockboxes in specific locations. The result of this analysis will be a cost-benefit calculation that trades off excessive mail float against the cost of additional lockboxes to arrive at the most profitable mix of lockbox locations.

A final issue is what to do with the residual checks that will continue to arrive at the company. Despite its best efforts, some customers will ignore all lockbox addresses and continue to send their checks directly to the company. When this happens, the controller can either process the checks as usual, using all of the traditional control points, or simply have the mail room staff put all of the checks into an envelope and mail them to the nearest lockbox. The latter approach is frequently the best because it allows a company to completely avoid all cash deposit procedures. The only case where the traditional cash processing approach may still have to be followed is when a company is in extreme need of cash and can deposit the funds more quickly by walking them to the nearest bank branch to deposit immediately. Otherwise, all checks should be routed through the lockbox.

The lockbox is especially useful in conjunction with the month-end close. If the accounting staff is extremely busy with closing tasks, it does not have to worry about depositing received checks at the local bank. Instead, the bank has already made the deposit of any lockbox receipts and has sent check copies to the company. If there is no time to post these check copies to the accounts receivable database, the accounting staff can simply set the bank's mailed copies to one side and wait to complete posting the cash until all closing tasks have been completed.

INSTALL A LOCKBOX TRUNCATION SYSTEM

What if checks come directly to a company, despite all efforts to have customers send them to a lockbox? Customers sometimes ignore lockbox instructions because they know there is some additional float time while the checks wend their way through the company and from there to the local bank. Also, depending on the check processing speed of the local bank, several additional days may be added to the float time. This can add up to substantial dollars of lost interest expense as well as reduced cash flow.

A solution is to use lockbox truncation. This is the process of converting a paper check into an electronic deposit. The basic process is to scan a check into a check reader, which scans the magnetic ink characters on the check into a vendor-supplied software package. The software sends this information to a third-party automated clearing house (ACH) processor, which typically clears payment in one or two days. The system has the additional benefit of eliminating deposit slips and the per-transaction deposit fees usually charged by banks. Also, not-sufficient-funds (NSF) fees are lower than if a regular check payment had been made, while NSFs can be redeposited at once.

An additional benefit of lockbox truncation is the handling of NSF checks. If such a check is returned by the bank, one can scan that check into the truncation system for processing through the ACH system. A third use of lockbox truncation is to enter into the system check information given to the company over the phone or fax by a customer. Rather than use the check scanner, one can manually punch in the information. This approach avoids the age-old "check is in the mail" excuse.

This service is now offered by many banks.

ACCESS ONLINE CHECK IMAGES FROM A LOCKBOX

The typical bank lockbox requires a wait of a few days during which the bank assembles all of the checks and related information it receives in the mail and sends it via the postal service to the company. It then arrives in the corporate mail room and eventually wends its way through the company to the accounts receivable department, where the checks are applied against invoices in the accounting system. This delay of a few days is irritating for the collections staff, which may be contacting customers about allegedly overdue accounts receivable that have already been received at the lockbox but about which the company is not yet aware.

The answer is to use lockboxes operated only by banks that scan the incoming checks and post the images on secure Web sites. This approach allows the collections staff to access check images immediately after checks arrive at the lockbox. Alternatively, the cash application staff accesses the images and records them in the accounting system as having been received, which the collections staff uses for receipt information instead.

The only downside to this best practice is the substantially reduced number of lockbox locations available, because only the larger (usually nationwide) and most technologically advanced banks offer this service.

CONSOLIDATE BANK ACCOUNTS

A time-consuming chore at the beginning of each month is to complete reconciliations between the bank statements for all of the company's bank accounts and the book balances it maintains for each of those accounts. For example, a retail store operation may have a separate bank account for each of hundreds of locations, each of which must be reconciled. Also, if it is the controller's policy to wait for all bank accounts to be reconciled before issuing financial statements, this can be the primary bottleneck operation that keeps financial statements from being issued in a timely manner. Finally, having many bank accounts raises the possibility that cash will linger in all of those accounts, resulting in less total cash being available for investment purposes. To use the previous example, if there are 100 retail stores and each has a bank account in which is deposited $5,000, then $500,000 has been rendered unavailable for investment.

The best way to resolve the multiaccount problem is to merge as many of them together as possible. To use the previous example, rather than give a bank account to each store, it may be possible to issue a fixed number of checks to each location, all of which will be drawn on the company's central bank account. This reduces the number of bank accounts from 100 to 1. If anyone feels there is a danger of someone fraudulently cashing a large check on the main bank account, this problem can be resolved by mandating a maximum amount for each check, above which the bank will not honor the check. By limiting the amount per check and the number of checks, this control effectively resolves any risk of a major fraud loss by consolidating all bank accounts. This is also an effective approach when acquiring another company, because its bank accounts can be merged into the existing account. In both cases, reducing the number of accounts also makes it much easier to track the cash balances in each account. Thus, account consolidation is an effective approach for improving accounting efficiency, managing cash flows, and speeding the closing process.

There are some problems to consider before consolidating bank accounts. One is that there may be automatic withdrawals taken out of an account. If the account is closed and merged into a different account, the automatic withdrawal will be terminated, resulting in an unhappy supplier who is no longer receiving any money. To avoid this problem, the transactions impacting each account must be reviewed to ensure that all automatic withdrawals are being shifted to the consolidated account. Also, there are legal reasons for keeping some accounts separate, such as a flexible spending account into which employee funds are deposited and from which a plan administrator withdraws funds. Finally, consolidating too many bank accounts may result in a difficult bank reconciliation chore. Sometimes it is easier to keep a small number of separate accounts, just to make reconciliations somewhat easier to untangle and resolve. However, with the exception of these few cases, it is generally possible to reduce the number of a company's bank accounts to a bare minimum, resulting in greater efficiency and more cash available for investment.

SUMMARY

This chapter discussed how account consolidation, lockbox services, and access to online bank account information can be used to increase the efficiency of the cash processing function and thereby improve the speed of the month-end close. Having now addressed efficiency improvements in all of the accounting functional areas, Chapter 13 turns to the role that the use of advanced computer systems can play in reducing the closing process to a single day.

ENDNOTE

1. Some sections of this chapter were adapted with permission from Chapter 6 of Bragg, *Accounting Best Practices*, 5th Edition (Hoboken, NJ: John Wiley & Sons, Inc., 2007).

13

Impact of Automation on the Closing Process

If consulting firms and software suppliers are to be believed, the only way to achieve a fast close is through the implementation of either packaged or custom software systems, which can automate all kinds of troublesome manual systems associated with the close. However, these systems are expensive (sometimes vastly so) and often require not months but actually years to install. Thus, in the interests of being fiscally prudent, this chapter on automation has been left until near the end of the book, in the hope that readers will implement the many other simple and less expensive changes recommended in earlier chapters before even considering automation.

Nonetheless, there is a place for automation in the closing process, especially for large, multidivision companies that must spend days collecting and consolidating division-level information. Even smaller companies can benefit from automation, but to such a smaller extent that their controllers should spend considerable time evaluating the cost and related benefits of each automation tool noted in this chapter.

In this chapter, the principles under which automation tools should be added to the closing process are covered, and then several types of automation are described, generally sorted in order by increasing levels of sophistication and expense.

PRINCIPLES OF FAST CLOSE AUTOMATION

Before considering any investment in automation, one should first be aware of several general principles of automation:

- *Do not automate a flawed process.* If an existing manual process already issues a large proportion of transaction errors, it is first necessary to alter the underlying process before even considering automation. Otherwise, any automation implementation will yield the same error-filled results, only faster.

- *Automate only if there is a cost-effective improvement in the closing process.* The latest software system may appear fabulous, with all of the latest bells and whistles, but what is the trade-off of its *total* cost (including software, implementation, testing, training, and ongoing support fees) against any net gains in performance? In many instances, a prudent controller will be well advised to retain a slightly longer closing interval rather than to make a major systems investment.

- *Focus on time reduction.* The intent of this book is to advise on how to close the books as fast as possible. With that goal in mind, place particular emphasis on those automation tools that are most likely to strip time out of the closing process. This goal is most easily reached by targeting any closing processes with substantial wait times. In particular, if it is possible to automate an entire task, then both the wait time and processing time associated with having a person tackle the same task will be eliminated.

- *Centralize accounting data.* One of the greatest banes of the multilocation company is trying to marshal the flow of accounting data into corporate headquarters in a reasonably efficient manner. This is most difficult if there are a multitude of disparate systems within the company. By focusing on the use of a small number of centralized systems, the closing process can be shortened.

IMPLEMENT MINOR PROGRAMMING CHANGES ON AN ONGOING BASIS

The first form of automation that the controller should consider is the use of minor programming changes on an ongoing basis. These changes tend to require minimal programming effort, involve modest procedural changes, and result in immediate and quantifiable reductions in the closing period. This approach compares well to the installation of extremely large systems, where both costs and resulting improvements are difficult to accurately quantify.

As an example, the clients of a consulting company each want different month-end reports describing hours worked. This can be a lengthy reformatting chore in the midst of the closing process, so the IT department designs a set of report formats from which the accounting staff can choose, containing varying levels of report detail. An even greater level of incremental automation would be to allow customers direct access to the various reports through an intranet site, so the accounting department no longer has to print any labor reports at all. Dozens of such improvements could be made to enhance the closing process, possibly individually saving only a few minutes of time each, but cumulatively resulting in a powerful, streamlined closing process.

The best way to use this approach is to list automation improvements as a task on the monthly closing checklist, to be reviewed by the project team as soon as the core closing tasks have been completed. The controller should discuss each proposed automation project with the IT manager to determine the extent of programming changes required and prioritize the automation request list based on the cost-benefit trade-off of each item.

AUTOMATE GENERAL LEDGER INTERFACES

Early versions of accounting software were designed on a modular basis, so that separate accounts payable, billing, inventory, payroll, and fixed asset modules accumulated information separately and required a manually initiated posting process to summarize and move transaction data into the general ledger. Not only did this call for additional processing steps in the midst of the month-end close, but it was also possible that the results of entire modules would not be posted at all or that late entries to a module would not be posted until the following month.

Many accounting software packages are now designed to automatically post subledger information straight into the general ledger without any manual interference by the accounting staff, thereby avoiding the problems just described. If this is not the case, review the software documentation to see if a trigger can be set in the underlying accounting tables that will automatically post module transactions to the general ledger. If not, consider modifying the software to do so, although this approach will cause problems if the company regularly updates to the most recent version of the accounting software, thereby eliminating any software code changes that may have been made. An alternative is to make a request to the software supplier through a users group, asking that automatic posting be added to the product in a forthcoming software release. Another alternative is to add the posting task to a list of activities in a workflow management software package (see the "Install a Workflow Management System" section), with direct links to the posting tasks within the accounting software; this approach will automatically force users to complete the posting task for every module.

INSTALL A WEB-BASED TIMEKEEPING SYSTEM

A major closing problem for those companies employing billable staff who work in the field is getting them to report their hours worked before the core closing period. Collecting time-worked data from those last few dilatory workers can seriously delay the creation of month-end billings and therefore the issuance of financial statements.

An excellent solution—and a rare case where technology can have a profound impact on the speed of the close—is the use of a Web-based timekeeping system. The best solution is a custom-designed system in which employees link hours billed to specific jobs, because the accounting staff can then sort the hours worked by job to rapidly create customer invoices. The author's company has used such a system for several years, even taking the concept to the point where the system prints backup documentation for hours worked that are then attached to invoices as proof of hours worked. These reports fit into one of three formats from which customers can choose:

1. Total hours worked by employee for the reporting period

2. Hours worked by employee for each day of the reporting period, laid out in a calendar format

3. Total hours worked on specific tasks by all employees during the reporting period

Thus, the use of a customized labor reporting system yields a great deal of reporting granularity. However, in many instances there is less need for such specificity. If so, several reporting systems are available that can either be purchased for sole use by a company or operated under an application service provider (ASP) model, where the supplier operates the software and attached database. Some examples are:

- ADP operates ezLaborManager on the ASP model. This is especially useful for those companies already processing their payroll through ADP's Pay eXpert product, because the time records feed directly into the payroll system.

- iEmployee's system is also on the ASP model and allows time to be charged to specific jobs. This system is designed to integrate with the payroll offerings of several outsourced payroll providers.

- Time Clock America sells a version on the ASP model, but it is not linked to any other payroll systems.

- Kronos's Central Suite takes the employee data entry concept considerably beyond just time data entry, also allowing employees to go online and alter their personal payroll information, view accrued vacation time and payroll information, submit leave requests, and enroll in various benefit programs.

The four offerings noted here are not the only ones available. Most of the full-service payroll providers appear to be developing this application or already have it, so be sure to conduct a thorough review of the latest offerings before making a selection. The key factor to consider when evaluating these systems is the ability to record hours for specific jobs, so the accounting staff can sort the resulting time records by job and use them to create invoices.

INSTALL A WORKFLOW MANAGEMENT SYSTEM

Consultants like to recommend the installation of an automated workflow management system to increase the speed of the closing process, because it monitors the flow of work through the accounting department, assigns tasks to employees, and ensures that procedures are followed in a specific order. Because the closing process is highly procedure driven, this would seem to be a good approach. However, such systems require a considerable software investment and substantial implementation costs. Just how good an investment is this system?

To answer the question, consider the reason why workflow management systems were developed. They are intended to allocate work among large numbers of employees handling very large transaction volumes, with work being automatically issued to those employees who are most capable of handling it while ensuring that wait times are minimized. However, the closing team is generally quite small, with each person already assigned to a specific set of tasks for which he or she is solely responsible. Thus, the performance of a small closing team would probably not be improved at all by a workflow management system. It could still be of use in a large corporate environment where the contribution of many people is needed in order to produce financial statements, but the controller would save a great deal of money by concentrating more effort or centralizing closing tasks with fewer people than by investing in a workflow management system.

If the decision is still made to invest in such a system, it is useful to understand some positive characteristics of the product. First, because it routes work to employees in a specific order, it can be designed to enforce the use of specific closing procedures. This can be a considerable benefit if the closing team is inexperienced or prone to making procedural mistakes. It is also useful if the controller is constantly tweaking closing procedures each month and wants the system to reflect the latest changes. Second, a workflow product records processing history, including who was assigned a task, how long the task took to complete, and the results of this action—all excellent information for a postmortem review of the closing process. This yields accurate information about process and wait time durations that can be used to constantly refine the closing process to achieve a faster close. Third, the controller can monitor the progress of each closing task in real time through the system to see who is handling each processing step at any given moment. If many people are using the system in distributed locations, this can be an excellent way to manage the close. Finally, the system can usually track which employees are away on vacation, taking training classes, and so on, and can automatically route work tasks to other backup staff to ensure that the closing schedule is not delayed.

In order to make a workflow management product an effective part of the closing process, it is useful to create interfaces to the underlying accounting system, so an employee can click on an assigned task and have the workflow system automatically launch the required program and access the specific document called for by the work step. Also, if closing tasks are being completed throughout a multidivision company, the workflow product must be accessible from all of these locations, which calls for real-time links to a central workflow database.

If there appears to be a use for a workflow management system to improve the closing process, go to the www.waria.com Web site for an overview of many workflow management suppliers. The site contains a supplier database, product descriptions, industry news, a bookstore, and a list of events. It is maintained by BPM-Focus. Other sites providing similar information about workflow are www.e-workflow.org, www.bpmi.org, and www.aiim.org.

INSTALL CONSOLIDATION SOFTWARE

One of the most justifiable automation tools related to the closing process is consolidation software. This standalone software package overlays a company's existing software and provides the following consolidation features:

- Consolidate financial data from multiple sources.

- Combine multiple currency data using a foreign exchange table.

- Centralize data from a broad array of chart of accounts configurations.

- Account for the percentage of equity ownership when determining consolidation rules.

- Allow some degree of drill-down inquiries into increasingly detailed levels of data.

Clearly, the main features of a consolidation system are oriented toward large, multidivision companies with complex equity holdings, especially those with international operations. Conversely, small or single-location companies have little need for consolidation software. Besides being expensive, the primary difficulty with consolidation software is the need for custom interfaces to other accounting systems within the company, which can be difficult to create and maintain.

Consolidation software is an integral part of the ERP software produced by Oracle, IBM, and SAP (see the "Install an Enterprise Resources Planning System" section in this chapter)

INSTALL A DATA WAREHOUSE

If a company is burdened with a large number of financial reporting systems in multiple locations, the closing staff will have a hard time collecting financial data within a reasonable period. A solution that retains the existing medley of systems while still providing the benefits of transaction centralization is to create a data warehouse. This is a database that acts as a central repository of key financial and other information, specifically designed for querying and reporting. The data stored in this warehouse is extracted from the regional accounting systems using either automated or manually triggered interfaces and cleaned with automated error-checking routines.

The querying portion of the data warehouse is enabled through a separate online analytical processing (OLAP) tool sold by several suppliers, such as SAS (www.sas.com), Oracle (www.oracle.com), and IBM (www.ibm .com). An OLAP tool is intended to provide fast query responses, cope with a broad range of logic questions, and make available a wide range of potential reporting formats. A properly installed OLAP can save some time during the closing process, because it can search through financial transactions for anomalies and bring them to the attention of the accounting staff, who then use the data warehouse to drill down through the flagged transactions to see what is wrong, correcting the problems faster than would otherwise be the case.

Once this system is implemented, the closing staff can rely on the data warehouse as its central information source, rather than divisional accounting systems. It can also be used as the central corporate report generator, which many users can access for a variety of reports. Furthermore, it can store data for longer periods than may be practical for the underlying accounting systems. Finally, a data warehouse allows access to users without giving them the ability to alter actual transactions, the primary versions of which are still stored elsewhere at the division level.

However, installing a data warehouse is a major undertaking, involving detailed analysis of data models throughout a company to ensure that the correct transactions are pulled from regional databases and forwarded to the central data repository. It requires numerous custom interfaces, as well as a high degree of ongoing maintenance to ensure that the interfaces still work and that the correct data is being centralized. Also, because the underlying mishmash of accounting systems has not been altered, there is still a high risk that divisional transaction error rates will be unacceptably high. Furthermore, if divisional accounting staffs are allowed to alter their charts of accounts, the system interfaces must constantly be revised to map these changes into the proper accounts in the data warehouse. Finally, the volume of data stored in a data warehouse calls for an industrial-strength database at its core, such as IBM's DB2, which is an expensive purchase.

For more information about data warehousing, access www.tdwi.org, which is operated by the Data Warehousing Institute.

INSTALL AN ENTERPRISE RESOURCES PLANNING SYSTEM

The most full-featured accounting system available is one that is both fully integrated with the computer systems running all parts of a company and installed in all company locations—the enterprise resources planning system (ERP). The most popular of these massive systems are sold by SAP and Oracle. These packages contain all of the consolidation functionality already noted for standalone consolidation software. In addition, an ERP system can also fully automate the elimination of intercompany receivables by identifying them in advance and having the software automatically consolidate them for review and elimination. Furthermore, the SAP version also tracks the consolidation status of all divisions using the software. Finally, the most important difference between ERP and consolidation software is that no custom interfaces are needed for an ERP system—all primary software systems in the company involve the same software, which is already fully integrated.

The downside of using ERP software is its massive cost and lengthy installation interval. There are numerous cases involving huge cost overruns and failed installations resulting in some jeopardy to a company's

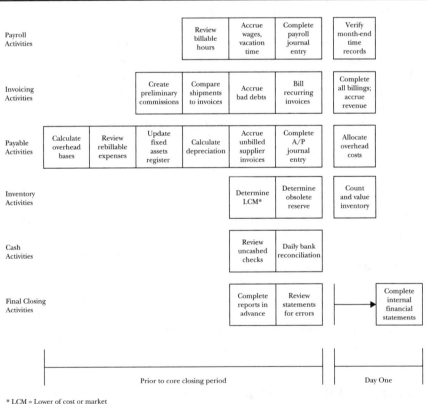

* LCM = Lower of cost or market

Exhibit 13.1   Modified Closing Timeline

ability to run its business. Consequently, justifying an ERP installation solely on the need to improve the speed of the close is a bad idea. There should be several other valid reasons justifying the installation. If the main justification for an ERP purchase is to improve the closing process, then consider buying standalone consolidation software instead.

The specific modules within each ERP system dealing with consolidations are the Oracle Global Consolidation System, and the SAP Consolidation Module. For more information about these systems, access www.oracle.com, or www.sap.com, respectively.

SUMMARY

The result of the added levels of automation to the closing process is shown in Exhibit 13.1. The greatest impact of automation was on final closing activities, where a currency conversion step (applicable only to those companies with foreign operations) was forcing the final generation of financial statements into a second day. By using an integrated currency conversion table in an ERP software package or a consolidation module, the conversion step can be eliminated, which brings the entire closing process following month-end to reside within a single day.

In the next two chapters, we turn away from the fast close process to consider two related issues—issuing financial reports to the Securities and Exchange Commission after the underlying financial statements have been completed, and the web of controls needed to ensure that the financial statements are accurate.

14

Closing the Books of a Public Company

OVERVIEW

A publicly held company must take one additional step in the issuance of its financial statements, which is to file those statements with the Securities and Exchange Commission (SEC). Unfortunately, the filing process requires the involvement of several outside parties, which makes it impossible to close the books in a single day. In fact, closing in a month can be considered a respectable accomplishment. In this chapter, we will note the extra steps required to file financial statements with the SEC, which is involved in the process, and what steps can be taken to shorten the time period. The initial steps in the process are shown in Exhibit 14.1, where completion of the financial statements trigger a great many additional activities that are described in the following sections. The time periods shown in the exhibit are estimates only, and can vary considerably in practice.

CONSTRUCTING THE SEC FILING

Financial statements and supporting disclosures must be filed by publicly held companies with the SEC on a quarterly basis. Those statements issued for the first, second, and third quarters of a company's fiscal year are called 10-Q reports, while the year-end report is called a 10-K report.

The 10-Q and 10-K reports include a company's basic financial statements, as well as a number of additional disclosures that greatly exceed the size of the statements. While a company may be accustomed to producing the financial statements in short order, it is the other parts of the SEC filings that can require a considerable amount of additional time to complete. Exhibit 14.2 shows a sampling of the additional contents of a 10-K report, as well as the likely timing of when each item can be completed.

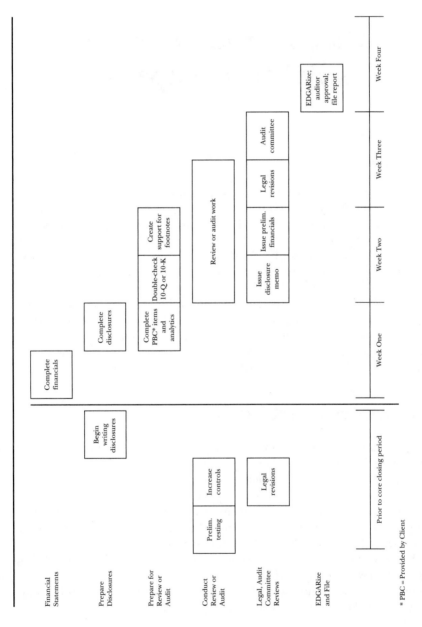

Financial
Statements

Prepare
Disclosures

Prepare for
Review or
Audit

Conduct
Review or
Audit

Legal, Audit
Committee
Reviews

EDGARize
and File

Prior to core closing period

Week One   Week Two   Week Three   Week Four

Complete
financials

Begin
writing
disclosures

Complete
disclosures

Complete
PBC* items
and
analytics

Double-check
10-Q or 10-K

Create
support for
footnotes

Review or audit work

Issue
disclosure
memo

Issue prelim.
financials

Legal
revisions

Audit
committee

Prelim.
testing

Increase
controls

Legal
revisions

EDGARize;
auditor
approval;
file report

* PBC = Provided by Client

Exhibit 14.1   Traditional SEC Filing Timeline

ITEM HEADER	DESCRIPTION	TIMING
Description of the business	Describes the company's general purpose, its history, business segments, customers, suppliers, sales and marketing operations, customer support, intellectual property, competition, and employees. It is designed to give the reader a grounding in what the company does and the business environment in which it operates.	Should be completed well before the financial statements, since the information it contains is general in nature, and is not dependent on any financial results.
Risk factors	An exhaustive compilation of all risks to which the company is subjected, and serves as a general warning to investors of what actions might negatively impact their investments in the company.	Should be completed well in advance, typically in cooperation with the company's general counsel.
Description of property	Describes the company's leased or owned facilities, including square footage, lease termination dates, and lease amounts paid per month.	All of this information can be readily compiled well in advance of the financial statements.
Legal proceedings	Describes current legal proceedings involving the company, and the company's estimate of the likely outcome of those proceedings.	Can complete an initial description of all legal proceedings before the end of the reporting period, and have the general counsel update it just prior to final issuance.
Market for company stock	Notes where the company's stock trades, the number of holders of record, and high and low closing prices per share, by quarter.	Most of the high–low bid prices require no updates, other than to drop the oldest quarter and add the newest. The number of shareholders of record requires input from the stock transfer agent, which should be available one day after the period-end.
Management's discussion and analysis (MD&A)	Involves multiple areas of required commentary, including opportunities, challenges, risks, trends, key performance indicators, future plans, and changes in revenues, cost of goods sold, other expenses, assets, and liabilities.	Requires much of the 10-K preparation time. Key performance indicators can include operational information, which may not be available until several days after the period-end. Also, the description of changes in accounts requires a detailed variance analysis that may not be practicable until after the financial statements have been completed. Thus, the variance analysis is a bottleneck.

Exhibit 14.2 Sampling of 10-K Report Contents

Footnotes to the financial statements	Includes all disclosures required by GAAP, including descriptions of acquisitions, discontinued operations, fixed assets, accrued liabilities, related-party transactions, income taxes, stock options, segment information, and many other possibilities, depending on the nature of a company's transactions.	Some GAAP disclosures change little between periods, and can be easily updated with a brief review prior to period-end. Other disclosures require some detail, such as fixed assets and accrued liabilities, and so are completed late in the 10-K preparation process.
Controls and procedures	A statement generally describing the company's system of internal controls, testing of controls, changes in controls, and management's conclusions regarding the effectiveness of controls.	This information is not contingent upon completion of the financial statements, and so can be completed well in advance of most of other parts of the 10-K.
Identification of control persons	Identifies executive officers, directors, promoters, and control persons.	Can be deferred and included in the annual proxy statement.
Executive compensation	Itemizes various types of compensation received by company executives.	Can be deferred and included in the annual proxy statement.
Security ownership of control persons and management	Notes the number of shares of all types owned or controlled by certain beneficial owners and management.	Can be deferred and included in the annual proxy statement.

Exhibit 14.2 (*Continued*)

It is apparent from the "timing" discussion in Exhibit 14.2 that all disclosures in a 10-K report can, to some extent, be completed prior to the end of the reporting period, with the notable exceptions of the Management Discussion and Analysis (MD&A) section and some financial statement footnotes.

The items described in Exhibit 14.2 are general SEC requirements that apply to all public companies. Companies in specialized industries, such as insurance or banking, must make extensive additional industry-specific disclosures in the financial statement footnotes. Also, certain activities require additional footnote disclosures, such as stock options, business combinations, pensions, and the use of variable-interest entities. The sum total of these disclosures can result in SEC filings having the approximate size of a small book.

Some smaller companies with minimal accounting support outsource the 10-Q and 10-K reports to SEC specialists, who create the entire reports. This solution works best for companies with small accounting staffs and relatively simple operations that require minimal disclosures. However, an SEC specialist is going to be flooded with work from multiple clients during quarterly reporting periods, so it can be difficult to obtain a completed report back from them in a timely manner. If this is a company's best alternative for constructing an SEC filing, then it should reserve a block of the specialist's time well in advance, and be absolutely certain to provide the person with all necessary items as of that date (usually the trial balance and an array of supporting documents, such as a calculation of earnings per share, the number of shares outstanding, any customers with sales exceeding 10 percent of total sales, and so on). In addition, the specialist is not as familiar with the company's operations as an insider would be, so the controller must carefully review the resulting 10-Q or 10-K report to ensure that no discussion items are incorrect or misleading.

Given the many additional items of information needed, it can take a number of days to complete the 10-Q and 10-K reports, especially if the company must wait in line for the services of an outside specialist to write them.

QUARTERLY AUDITOR REVIEWS AND AUDITS

The company's external auditors must conduct a review of the 10-Q reports, and a full audit of the 10-K report (henceforth, we will describe both reviews and audits as "audits"). These audits represent the longest block of time between creating the initial set of financial statements and filing reports with the SEC, and so are worth considerable attention from the perspective of a fast close. The goal is to shrink the length of the audit work.

The duration of an audit will depend on the complexity of the company's financial records, the strength of its control systems, the personnel assigned to the work by both the company and its auditors, the preceding testing work already completed by the auditors, the accuracy of the 10-Q or

10-K report, and the accuracy of the underlying records. The following bullet points note ways to alter these variables to achieve the shortest possible audit:

- *Maximize auditor staff power.* Auditors must complete a clearly defined series of review or audit steps that require a specific amount of time. It is not usually possible to reduce the total number of work hours involved, but it may be possible to influence the auditors to assign the maximum number of their staff to the work, in order to compress more work into fewer days. This concept can be taken only so far—assigning 100 auditors to a review that requires 100 hours does *not* mean that the review will be completed in one hour! The countervailing pressure from the auditors is that, if they have multiple publicly held clients, they must spread a limited number of auditors over multiple companies. However, if the company's audit committee is willing to apply pressure on the auditors, this can at least result in a fully staffed audit. If the auditor agrees to maximize staffing, this will only be for a limited amount of time that is carefully scheduled, so the company must have its records completely ready for an audit on the scheduled audit start date.

- *Retain experienced auditors.* A key factor in the efficiency of an audit is the experience level of the auditors assigned to work on the company's audit. This does not mean that the company should insist on having no one below the level of partner conduct its audits! However, the controller should have a considerable interest in seeing the same auditors return time and again. An auditor who has a long history of reviewing a company's controls and records is much more efficient than someone who has no knowledge of the company. Thus, the company should express continuing interest in retaining existing auditors on an ongoing basis. In addition, if a new auditor is assigned to the next audit, volunteer to give him a training session before the period-end close, which can involve a tour of the facilities, meetings with key accounting personnel, preliminary transaction tests, and so forth. The goal is to increase new auditor familiarization with the company before the audit begins.

- *Maximize audit support by the company.* If the auditors are willing to maximize their staffing of an audit, then the company should do so as well. There is a significant amount of audit support work to be done, such as completing analytical reviews, pulling underlying files from records, and assisting with receivables confirmations. If anything, the controller should assign too much staff to support the auditors, to ensure that these tasks are completed promptly. Ultimately, the goal of overstaffing is to ensure that the auditors complete their work within the scheduled time period, so that no auditors have to be released from the company's audit and sent to their next scheduled audit, thereby prolonging the completion of the company's audit.

- *Encourage preliminary testing.* There are a number of tests that auditors can complete prior to the year-end audit; for example, they can review debt, equity, and fixed asset detail records a month or so in advance of the audit, which leaves them with minimal roll-forward work to complete during the actual audit. The company should encourage this preliminary testing, since it reduces the length of the audit. This solution is of minimal value for quarterly reviews, since auditors are not conducting such extensive testing during those times.

- *Delay the audit.* The entire SEC filing process may actually be completed sooner if the audit is delayed a few days. This is because, as just noted, the auditors can assign a maximum number of staff to an audit for only a limited period of time—and if the company has not had sufficient time to prepare materials for the auditors, then audit staff time will be wasted, thereby prolonging the audit. Thus, despite the seemingly reverse logic of delaying the start of the audit, it can actually reduce the total length of the filing process.

- *Increase control strength.* If audit testing determines that there are errors in the underlying accounting records, the auditors must spend more time reviewing an even larger sample of accounting records. This requires more time by both the auditors (who are the scarce resource) and the company's staff, who must pull the additional records for the auditors to review. Consequently, it pays off in reduced audit time if the company installs the strongest possible controls over accounting transactions. In particular, if the audit team finds errors in a particular set of transactions, then the controller should be absolutely certain that new controls have eliminated the bulk of those errors by the time of the next audit. Increasing control strength may require significant in-house staffing, so the controller must weigh the incremental cost of new controls against the corresponding reduction in audit duration.

- *Double-check the 10-Q or 10-K report.* Auditors do not like to waste time reviewing multiple versions of SEC reports, since it turns them into high-priced document reviewers, and also extends the duration of the audit. Instead, once the first draft of a document is prepared, have a second person review it in great detail. In particular, verify that historical information matches what was reported in earlier SEC filings. If the reviewer finds multiple errors, it even makes sense to have yet another person conduct an additional review, to ensure that *all* mistakes are rooted out before the auditors see a draft.

- *Complete supporting documentation for footnotes.* Besides the financial statements, the 10-Q and 10-K reports contain extensive discussions of the company's financial results in the MD&A section. The auditors will review the MD&A section in considerable detail, and will want proof of various assertions made by the company. For example, if the company states that its consulting segment comprises 75% of total company revenues, then the company should have a spreadsheet prepared that proves this. By creating a standard package of supporting documentation for the auditors, a company can shave some additional time from its audit.

Even if a company implements *all* of the preceding recommendations, there is still a limit on how short the audit process can become. It is scheduled by a third party that faces conflicting priorities with multiple clients, which indicates that there will be auditor shortages, and most of the audit work must be conducted by the auditors. For all of these reasons, and despite all the work a controller may complete to initially prepare financial statements in a single day, auditing of the results may not be completed for weeks thereafter.

QUARTERLY LEGAL REVIEW

A company's legal counsel must review the 10-Q and 10-K reports to ensure that all legally mandated disclosures and supporting schedules have been included. This review also searches for incorrect or unsupportable statements made in the disclosures. This is an extremely important service, so the attorneys must have sufficient time for a proper review.

Fortunately, the attorneys are not concerned with the accuracy of the financial statements; for example, they will not comb through an SEC filing to verify that the percentage increase in sales from the previous reporting period is correct. The attorneys leave that task for the auditors. Thus it is quite possible to issue a review copy of the 10-Q or 10-K report to the attorneys before the auditors have completed their work. Any changes made by the attorneys can then be incorporated into the latest draft of the 10-Q or 10-K that the auditors are reviewing.

Thus the quarterly legal review can be completed at the same time as the audit, which removes it from the filing timeline as a bottleneck.

OFFICER CERTIFICATION

Section 906 of the Sarbanes-Oxley Act stipulates that the Chief Executive Officer (CEO) and Chief Financial Officer (CFO) of a publicly held company must issue a written statement with every financial statement released, certifying that the information contained within it presents fairly, in all material respects, its financial condition and results of operations. If these officers issue such statements knowing that the financial statements do not present such information, then they can be fined up to $5 million and/or be imprisoned up to 20 years.

Given the severity of these penalties, it should be no surprise that the CEO and CFO may want to spend extra time reviewing the financial statements before agreeing to file them with the SEC. This is not really a significant problem, because both officers can review the financial statements while the auditors are conducting their review. This gives both people at least a week in which to read and comment on the financial statements before there is any possibility of filing the statements. Thus they are not a bottleneck in the closing process.

If there have been problems in the past with financial statement accuracy, the CEO and CFO may be especially careful about issuing their respective approvals. If this is the case, copy them on the results of all control reviews by the internal audit staff. This allows the officers to verify that various control problems are being identified and corrected, and should increase their confidence in the accuracy of the financial statements.

AUDIT COMMITTEE APPROVAL

The company's audit committee must also give its formal approval of the 10-Q and 10-K filings. The committee may consent to approving an early version of either report, but by far the most common scenario is to send them the final version, after all changes have been made. This is a reasonable request by the audit committee, since it doesn't want to approve reports that may be subsequently changed. Since this approval stands as a discrete step between the auditor review and EDGARizing (as discussed next), it is a bottleneck that lengthens the filing time.

The audit committee approval meeting must be set multiple days in advance, in order to coordinate the schedules of the committee members. The committee generally wants to see the 10-Q or 10-K report at least 24 hours before the meeting, to insure they have sufficient time for a proper review. The group then discusses the report during a conference call, the controller or an assistant notes all recommendations made during the meeting, and the accounting staff then creates an updated version of the report following the call.

It is extremely difficult to reduce the audit committee's timeline, but there are a few ways to achieve minor time reductions. One possibility is to issue a disclosure memo to the committee members well before they see the financial statements. A disclosure memo itemizes the accounting issues that the company is addressing in the current financial statements, such as a change in accounting method. If the committee members are aware of these issues in advance, they will be less likely to address them again during the committee meeting, and even less likely to request changes in the financial statements. An example of a disclosure memo is shown in Chapter 15, Controls for Financial Reporting.

Another possibility is to issue the financial statements to the committee members before the supporting footnotes and disclosures are released.

The financial statements are usually complete several days earlier, so the committee can see them as soon as possible. Again, this leaves less material for discussion during the formal audit committee meeting.

Finally, the committee members can be encouraged to contact the controller prior to the committee meeting to discuss any changes they would like to see in the financial statements. This reduces the length of the committee meeting, and also allows the accounting staff sufficient time to update the reports at their leisure before the meeting.

While these improvements can incrementally reduce the length of the audit committee's approval process, the main issue is the formal committee meeting itself. As such it must be scheduled well in advance and is difficult to change, and hence is a bottleneck in the SEC filing process.

EDGARIZING

The SEC accepts 10-Q and 10-K filings through its Electronic Data Gathering, Analysis, and Retrieval (EDGAR) system. There are various formats in which the reports can be submitted to the system, of which HyperText Markup Language (HTML) is the most common, and Extensible Markup Language (XML) is soon to be required. Companies filing their reports with the SEC almost always forward them to a firm specializing in the conversion of their reports into HTML or XML (known as *EDGARizing*); the specialist converts the statements to the required format and then files them with the SEC on behalf of the company.

A company's auditors usually insist on reviewing its EDGARized reports prior to filing, and in fact will not allow the statements to be filed at all until this review has taken place. This can result in several rounds of corrections, as the auditors require changes that the EDGARizing firm must make. These extra iterations are expensive, both in terms of auditor and EDGARizing fees and the extra time required to file the reports with the SEC. Thus, it is well worth the effort to conduct a detailed review of the 10-Q or 10-K report before forwarding it to the EDGARizing firm.

Quarterly and annual filings usually arrive at an EDGARizing firm from multiple companies at about the same time, which can create a considerable backlog, and lengthens the time required to file. The best way around this problem is to file well before the SEC-mandated due dates, so that there are fewer competing filings. Another option is to retain the services of a smaller, local EDGARizing firm, which will be more likely to put greater emphasis on completing a company's filings in a timely manner.

SUMMARY

The preceding chapters have described a process whereby the financial statements can be completed in a single day. In this chapter, we have

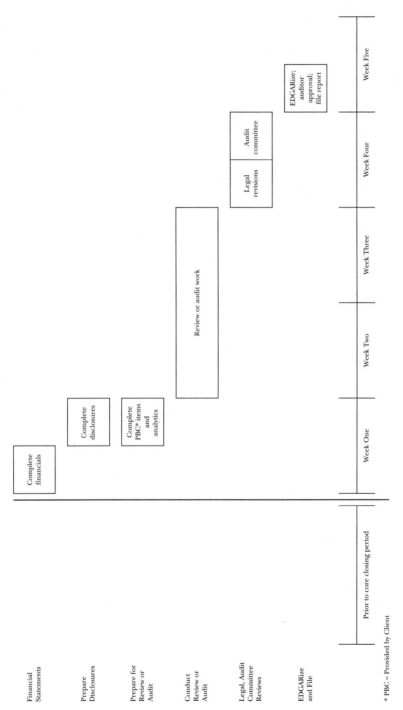

* PBC = Provided by Client

Exhibit 14.3   Modified SEC Filing Timeline

pointed out the impossibility of also filing the same statements with the SEC by the end of that single day. In fact, filing within a month may be difficult to achieve. This vast expansion of the one-day goal is primarily caused by the mandatory auditor review at the end of each quarter, and the full audit at the end of each fiscal year. These reviews and audits are under the control of an outside audit firm, which has ultimate control over the speed of the process. Though we have noted numerous methods in this chapter for reducing the filing process somewhat, the involvement of outside auditors presents a significant hurdle that cannot be avoided. The revised timeline, incorporating the changes noted in this chapter, is shown in Exhibit 14.3.

The other chapters of this book showed how to issue financial statements in a single day; a key factor in this accomplishment was keeping all facets of the closing process under the company's direct control. However, since the SEC filing process involves multiple outsiders—auditors, attorneys, the audit committee, and the EDGARizing firm—the company loses so much control over the process that it can shave only one week from the filing timeline.

15

Controls for Financial Reporting

OVERVIEW

Every other chapter in this book is concerned with compressing the time period needed to produce financial statements. However, excessive attention to a fast close can result in the elimination of those controls that keep the financials from being misstated. In this age of Sarbanes-Oxley, where the managers of public companies can be held personally responsible for the accuracy of their financial statements, controls play an increasingly important role.

Given these concerns, this chapter runs against every other chapter in this book by describing a number of manual controls that *slow down* the closing process, simply because they require more work to be done to ensure that the financial statements have not been misstated. A company's management team needs to determine how many of these controls it can afford to eliminate, balanced against the offsetting risk of creating inaccurate financial statements. A more conservative group will implement every control noted here, while others may opt for fewer controls.

CONTROLS FOR FINANCIAL REPORTING

The general closing process does not vary much by company, and generally follows the process flow shown in Exhibit 15.1. Public companies must endure a number of additional steps, including a quarterly audit review, approval of the audit committee, and conversion of the financial statements into a format readable by the SEC's EDGAR filing system (as more fully described in Chapter 14). These extra steps can add weeks to the closing process, as well as several additional controls.

The controls noted in the exhibit are described at greater length, next, in sequence from the top of the flowchart to the bottom.

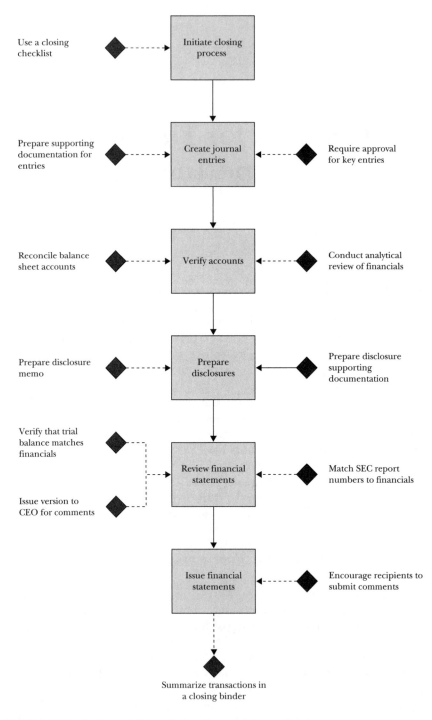

Exhibit 15.1   System of Controls for Financial Reporting

- *Use a closing checklist.* It is mandatory to follow a closing checklist when closing the books. Given the complexity of the closing process, this is the only way to ensure that every closing step has been completed. In addition, the financial statement preparer should initial each closing step as completed. Further, a supervisor should then review the checklist and all underlying journal entries to ensure that the close has been properly completed, and also initial the checklist. A sample closing checklist is shown in Exhibit 15.2, while a more complete version is shown in Appendix A.

- *Prepare supporting documentation for all complex manual entries.* Any journal entry that requires a complex calculation, such as an obsolescence

---

Prior to Month-End
- [ ] Review and correct sub ledger transactions throughout the month
- [ ] Complete the bank reconciliation every day
- [ ] Update inventory obsolescence reserve
- [ ] Determine the lower of cost or market
- [ ] Calculate overhead allocation bases
- [ ] Bill recurring invoices
- [ ] Review preliminary re billable expenses
- [ ] Update the bad debt reserve
- [ ] Review preliminary billable hours
- [ ] Accrue interest expense
- [ ] Determine pension plan funding
- [ ] Determine flexible spending account funding
- [ ] Accrue unpaid wages
- [ ] Accrue unused vacation time
- [ ] Accrue travel expenses
- [ ] Reconcile asset and liability accounts
- [ ] Update the fixed asset register
- [ ] Calculate depreciation
- [ ] Compile preliminary commissions
- [ ] Review financial statements for errors
- [ ] Complete selected financial reports

During Core Closing Period
- [ ] Ensure inventory cutoff
- [ ] Complete all employee time records
- [ ] Count and value inventory

- [ ] Enter late supplier invoices
- [ ] Complete month-end invoicing
- [ ] Accrue revenue for unbilled jobs
- [ ] Accrue commissions on month-end invoices
- [ ] Accrue royalties
- [ ] Convert division results to reporting currency
- [ ] Map division results to corporate chart of accounts
- [ ] Eliminate inter company transactions
- [ ] Review preliminary financial statements
- [ ] Adjust errors at corporate and division levels
- [ ] Accrue income tax liability
- [ ] Finalize and issue financial statements

Deferred Beyond Core Closing Period
- [ ] Defer invoice mailing
- [ ] Defer invoicing of re billable expenses
- [ ] Complete bank reconciliation based on final bank statement
- [ ] Calculate and review closing metrics
- [ ] Determine improvement targets for next month
- [ ] Initiate programming changes for further improvements
- [ ] Review accounting systems for standardization opportunities
- [ ] Update closing procedures

Exhibit 15.2   Sample Closing Checklist

reserve or an overhead allocation, must be supported by extensive written documentation.

- *Require approval for key entries.* Key journal entries are those that are at the highest risk of error, or which have a significant monetary impact on the financial statements. These entries should be carefully reviewed and approved by a supervisor, who should initial the closing checklist.

- *Reconcile all significant balance sheet accounts.* Categorize all balance sheet accounts by risk that they may contain errors, and by size of potential errors. Higher-risk accounts typically involve manual entries and complex transactions. Those accounts scoring highest must be fully reconciled before the financial statements are issued. Accounts with lower scores can be completed prior to the end of the reporting period, even if this means that additional entries will be added to the accounts subsequent to the reconciliation. This review process should require the use of a checklist of accounts to be reconciled, and a formal review of the reconciliations by a second person.

- *Conduct an analytical review of the balance sheet, income statement, and cash flow statement.* This is a spreadsheet-based comparison of the balance in an account as compared to the same balance in a previous period, to see if the change is reasonable. For example, this can include a comparison of the first quarter of this year to the first quarter of last year, with a detailed explanation required for all variances greater than 10% and $25,000. Another option is to annualize the current partial-year results and compare them to the preceding full-year results. Examples of analytical reviews by customer and by account are shown in Exhibit 15.3. Note how "not applicable" is used as an explanation whenever the period-over-period analysis is too small to be worthy of any investigatory time.

- *Prepare a disclosure memo to the disclosure committee.* It is useful to have a group of experts in financial disclosures review key accounting issues once a quarter. An excellent vehicle for this review is a disclosure memo, in which the controller itemizes key accounting issues for their review. The disclosure committee should include an SEC expert, corporate counsel, and the CEO. It may also be useful to send a copy to the company's audit manager. A highly abbreviated disclosure memo is shown in Exhibit 15.4.

- *Prepare supporting documentation for all footnote disclosures.* Footnote disclosures that are read by the public put the company at risk if they are inaccurate, so have a complete set of supporting documents that show exactly how the information in each disclosure was derived.

- *Match all SEC report numbers to the financial statements.* A person besides the preparer of the quarterly or annual SEC report should carefully

Customer Analysis	Quarter 2	Quarter 1	% Change	$ Change	Explanation
IBM	$10,500	$10,100	+4%	+$300	Not applicable
Interior department	15,900	23,500	−32%	+7,600	23 additional billable staff
Lockheed Martin	28,500	19,500	−46%	−900	ABC project was canceled
Balance Sheet Analysis					
Accounts receivable	$42,000	$36,000	+17%	+$6,000	In line with sales increase
Fixed assets	14,500	10,000	+45%	+4,500	Acquired airplane
Accounts payable	10,000	9,500	5%	+500	Not applicable
Notes payable	8,000	3,500	129%	+4,500	Acquired airplane
Income Statement Analysis					
Sales – consulting	$85,000	$73,000	+16%	+$12,000	Net increase in IRS project
Employee benefits	2,500	2,000	+25%	+500	Health insurance increase
Marketing	700	2,100	−67%	−1,400	Trade show in first quarter
Salaries	43,000	42,000	+2%	+1,000	Not applicable
Travel	250	950	−74%	−700	Travel to/from trade show

Exhibit 15.3   Analytical Review Examples

compare all numbers in the document to the underlying trial balance and other supporting materials. In addition, this reviewer should compare the prior period comparisons in the SEC report to the actual prior period reports. By doing so, the company should catch and correct the bulk of all errors, thereby hopefully yielding a clean review of the document by the auditors.

- *Issue preliminary version of financial statements to CEO for comments.* The CEO is required to sign off on financial statements that are included in SEC filings. Given this person's vested interest in the financial statements, it makes sense to issue a preliminary copy to him well before the financials are ready for issuance, so that any concerns can be addressed well in advance. This is also a weak control, since the CEO may spot an accounting problem or (more likely) an inaccurate disclosure.

This memo notes the accounting treatment used for a variety of items in the third-quarter 10-Q filing. The memo is being sent to you, because our internal controls procedure requires that you review it *and respond back* by e-mail that you have received and reviewed it. Key accounting disclosures are:

1. *Intangible asset/goodwill impairment.* We test for goodwill impairment at the subsidiary level, which we must do at least annually, as well as whenever an impairment event occurs. The goodwill assigned to each subsidiary and its annual testing date are as follows:

   • Subsidiary A, $1.3 million, 4th quarter

   • Subsidiary B, $1.9 million, 4th quarter

   • Subsidiary C, $4.2 million, 4th quarter

   All impairment tests fall into the next quarter. Given current cash flows, there is no evidence of impairment at this time.

2. *Revenue accruals.* Subsidiary A has a number of fixed-fee contracts, for which it has historically used the percentage-of-completion method to record revenue. However, the SEC has stipulated that public companies must use the proportional method instead (which is based on milestones achieved). We have reviewed the proportional method with our auditors following the last year-end audit, and documented a standard procedure for revenue recognition.

3. *MD&A topics.* Since we are acquiring companies with few material assets, a considerable proportion of the prices we pay must be allocated to intangible assets. This allocation is provided to us by third-party valuation firms. These firms are slow in providing final reports, so we are forced to initially estimate the amount of the purchase price allocated between goodwill and intangible assets, and then create a second (adjusting) entry once the valuation report is received. This can result in some inaccuracy in the amount of amortization reported for a short interval.

   Subsidiary B has just brought up the risk of high fuel prices on the operation of its airplanes, and the resulting decline in profitability of its data collection activities. The subsidiary's staff is preparing a risk disclosure concerning this issue.

4. *Assessment and evaluation of operational or legal risks.* A former business partner of Subsidiary C has filed suit against the company, related to alleged amounts owed to it from a deal several years ago, and seeking relief of $1,000,000. Since the case has been thrown out of court twice before, we do not assign any probability to a monetary settlement.

Exhibit 15.4   Disclosure Memo Example

- *Verify that the trial balance matches the financial statements.* It is entirely possible that a late journal entry will alter the trial balance, which can be a major problem if the financial statements have already been printed. Accordingly, this control should be used near the end of the financial statement process. Before issuing any statements, make sure that the trial balance still matches the financial statements. This can be a particular problem when the accounting staff has recently altered the format of the financials, since the new format may inadvertently not include some accounts, or include some accounts more than once.

- *Encourage financial statement recipients to submit comments.* The company managers who receive the financial statements may have particular insights into company operations that the accounting staff is not aware of. If so, it makes sense when issuing financial statements to these people to append a note requesting that they provide comments on any issues that appear to be incorrect or questionable. Though not a strong control, it may occasionally provide warning of a reporting problem.

- *Summarize all supporting transactions in a closing binder.* It is not acceptable to prepare a detailed justification for a journal entry, and then lose the justification. Instead, collect all supporting documentation for all entries made during a reporting period, and organize them into a closing binder. Ideally, each page of the binder should be indexed back to a table of contents, so that anyone can easily locate materials within the binder.

The controls noted above must be used for the quarterly filings of public companies, since these entities are most concerned with avoiding errors. There may be some opportunity to reduce the level of control over the other months of the year, since these other financial statements are generally used only internally.

While the controls noted above form the core controls for financial statement preparation, also consider using the following two controls occasionally that are related to spreadsheets:

- *Lock and archive spreadsheets used for journal entries.* There is a considerable risk within the accounting department that any spreadsheets used to derive journal entries will simply be wiped clean in the following month and used again, which eliminates any evidence (besides printed matter) of how journal entries were derived. To avoid this issue, have the accounting staff copy formulas into a new spreadsheet for each month, and lock the old spreadsheets to avoid reuse.

- *Periodically review the structure of supporting spreadsheets.* Electronic spreadsheets are highly subject to errors, and so must be regularly reviewed to ensure that they still operate as intended. Accordingly, there should be at least an annual review of all spreadsheets used to compile the financial statements. This review should encompass a verification of all calculations used, references to other spreadsheets, and the ranges used to summarize data.

A procedure listing the basic steps needed to create the financial statements, while incorporating many of the controls noted here, is shown in Exhibit 15.5. A more expansive series of procedures is available in Appendix B.

Of all the controls noted above, the use of a closing checklist is by far the most important. The closing process is much too complex for a controller to keep organized in an informal manner, so proper documentation of the process flow is critical. It is also mandatory to retain sufficient explanatory documentation of every journal entry made, and to organize this information into a closing binder. Otherwise, it is impossible to determine why entries have been made. Finally, it is extremely useful to reconcile accounts and perform at least high-level analytical scrutiny. These reviews may find a major error in the financial statements that would otherwise have led to significantly inaccurate financial statements.

Policy/Procedure Statement   Retrieval No.: FINL-01
Subject: Financial Statement Creation

1. PURPOSE AND SCOPE

This procedure is used by the accounting department to close the books each month and issue financial statements.

2. PROCEDURES

2.1. Initiate Closing Process

1. Update the closing checklist from the previous month.

2. Assign responsibilities for items on the checklist.

3. Call an accounting team meeting to discuss responsibilities and projected deliverable due dates.

2.2. Create Journal Entries

1. Prepare supporting documentation for all journal entries. A supervisor should review and initial all journal entries to indicate his approval.

2. The general ledger accountant should enter all journal entries in the accounting system, and maintain a log of all entries made.

[Note: Journal entries will be required for many of the following steps]

2.3. Complete Accounts Payable Closing Activities

1. Review the re billable expenses account in the general ledger and verify that expense reports have been received for all weeks in which travel has been approved. If expense reports have not been recorded, contact employees and request that the expense reports be sent to the accounting department at once.

2. Ask the travel department to forward a list of employees who have gone on approved trips during the month, including the airfare costs as processed by the travel department. Based on the departure and return dates on these airfares, calculate per-diem lodging and meal charges. Calculate the travel expense accrual based on this information, less the amount of any expense reports received from employees.

3. If supplier invoices arrive during the core closing period and they have not already been accrued, enter them as expenses in the reporting period.

4. Review the royalty checklist to verify the amount of royalty expense to record based on billed revenues. Record this amount as an account payable in the reporting period.

2.4. Complete Billing Closing Activities

1. Print the recurring invoices report from the subscription database and forward it to the sales manager for review and approval. Once returned, make any changes noted by the sales manager. Then set the accounting system's database date to the next reporting period and print the recurring invoices. Reset the system date to the current reporting period. Mail the invoices to customers.

2. Discuss the accounts receivable aging with the credit manager, highlighting prospective collection problems with newer invoices, as well as the status of older unpaid ones. Adjust the bad debt reserve to reflect the anticipated bad debts. As a cross-check, stratify the aging report by 30-day time buckets and apply the historical bad debt loss rate to each bucket. Compare the result to the bad debt reserve and adjust the reserve accordingly.

3. Verify that all shipments have been made and that employees whose hours are billable have completed their entries of hours worked into the timekeeping system. Process invoices. Forward them to another clerk for error checking, and revise as necessary. Mail to customers.

4. If there are jobs for which hours have been worked but no invoice is to be issued, summarize the billable rates and hours to determine the amount that would have been billed. Adjust this amount downward if it would exceed any fixed billable total for the job, and create a journal entry to record the accrued revenue.

2.5. Complete Cost Accountant Closing Activities

1. Print the "where used" report to spot any unused inventory that is no longer included in any bills of materials. Meet with the Materials Review Board to review these items and determine their disposition. Adjust the inventory obsolescence reserve based on this information.

2. Obtain a listing of raw material market prices from the purchasing department and compare these prices to the costs at which they are recorded for in-house inventory items. If the recorded cost exceeds market value, prepare a journal entry that writes down their value to market.

3. Verify with the controller what activities are being used as allocation bases, and then compile the latest activity information for these items. Compare the activity totals to the totals from the last reporting period for consistency, and report any anomalies to the controller.

4. Send an e-mail to the receiving manager, verifying that inventory receipts will be recorded in the proper accounting period. Conduct a spot-check of receiving records on the morning of the core closing period to ensure that this is the case.

5. If cycle counts of the inventory reveal accuracy levels exceeding 95%, no formal month-end inventory count is necessary—instead, print the inventory report, calculate metrics, and compare the results to the metrics from the prior three periods. If they are similar, close the inventory module. If not, conduct further investigation into significant changes.

2.6. Complete Fixed Asset Closing Activities

1. Ensure that all accounts payable have been recorded in the current accounting period. Then print the general ledger to see what assets have been added during the period. Transfer this information to the fixed assets register and store supporting purchase documentation in the fixed assets binder, sorted by asset type.

2. Print the depreciation report in the fixed assets register. Compare the depreciation expense in this report to the recurring depreciation entry, and adjust the recurring entry to match the report.

2.7. Complete Payroll Closing Activities

1. Print the timekeeping report and see who has not recorded hours for the billing period. Send them reminder messages to do so.

2. Based on the monthly payroll reports, determine the amount of employee 401k deductions that must be shifted to the independent 401k provider, and record this cash transfer.

3. Based on the monthly payroll reports, determine the amount of employee flexible spending account (FSA) deductions that must be shifted to the FSA administration company, and record this cash transfer.

4. Compile unpaid hours worked for hourly employees and multiply these hours by standard hourly rates to arrive at the unpaid wages accrual.

5. Update the unused vacation time spreadsheet with any pay rate changes, additional accrued vacation time, and used vacation time. Compare the result to the accrued vacation expense balance, and adjust the balance as necessary.

6. Calculate commissions based on final invoicing. Forward the calculations to the sales manager for review, and accrue the amount of the commissions.

2.8. Complete General Ledger Closing Activities

1. Scan sub ledger transactions for obvious anomalies in terms of the size of transactions or the accounts to which they are charged, and investigate as necessary.

2. Calculate the number of days over which debt has been outstanding during the month, multiply it by the daily interest rate, and record the monthly interest expense based on this information.

3. Verify that the currency valuations in the currency conversion table match currency rates at month-end, and process the currency conversion.

4. Verify that no chart of accounts changes have occurred during the month, and verify that the control totals submitted by the divisional accounting departments match the mapped totals recorded by the consolidation software. If not, search for unmapped accounts and correct as necessary.

5. Obtain the income tax accrual from the corporate tax manager and record the entry.

6. Once printed bank statements are received from the bank, verify that they match the Internet-based statements already used for daily reconciliations, and file the statements.

2.9. Verify Accounts

1. Conduct an analytical review of all accounts in the chart of accounts. This should be a comparison of the current year-to-date balance against the preceding year's year-to-date balance. Review in detail any variances that have experienced both a 10+% change and a $25,000+ change.

2. Reconcile all balance sheet accounts having a balance greater than $25,000.

3. Review all revenue recognition calculations and related accruals.

2.10. Prepare Disclosures

1. Prepare disclosure supporting documentation for all footnotes and items listed in the Management Discussion and Analysis section, showing how all numbers were derived.

2. Prepare a disclosure memo for the disclosure committee, itemizing all accounting issues encountered during the past quarter, and noting how each one was treated in the financial statements.

3. Issue the disclosure memo to the disclosure committee, with a request to acknowledge receipt.

2.11. Review Financial Statements

1. Verify that the trial balance matches the financial statements.

2. Match the financial statement numbers against the numbers listed in any SEC quarterly or annual report.

3. Issue a preliminary version of the financial statements to the CEO for review.

4. Have the audit committee review and approve any financial statements being issued to the SEC.

5. Have the auditors review and approve any financial statements being issued to the SEC.

2.12. Issue Financial Statements

1. Convert the financial statements to XML formatting.

2. Submit the financial statements to the SEC.

3. Issue subsidiary-level financial statements to the managers of those divisions, as well as complete financial statements to the CEO and CFO.

2.13. Summarize Transactions in a Closing Binder

1. Assemble all backup materials used to create the financial statements.

2. Put the closing checklist in front of this material and sort the material to match the sequence listed on the checklist.

3. Label each page of the supporting material with the index number shown on the closing checklist.

4. Label the binder with the date of the reporting period.

5. Store the binder in the accounting archives room.

Exhibit 15.5   Financial Statement Creation Procedure

SUMMARY

If a company is publicly held, then it must be extremely careful to issue accurate financial statements. If not, it can be considered to have significant control problems, which can result in substantial additional systems analyses, auditing, and potentially even the restatement of its reported results. To a lesser degree, the same concerns arise for private companies, if they must issue results to their creditors or shareholders. To improve the odds of issuing correct financial statements, a multi layered series of controls can be implemented. These controls can be time-consuming, and as such may be more rigorously enforced at quarter-end or year-end, but less so during other periods. There is a trade-off between the speed of issuing financial statements and ensuring that they are correct, so expect some publication delay if a full suite of controls are installed.

16

Ongoing Improvements in the Closing Process

Even if you religiously implement all of the suggestions made in the preceding chapters, this does not mean that there is no further room for improvement. On the contrary, if the achievement of a fast close is treated as a one-time project, there will inevitably be a continual degradation of the process once the project has been completed; inefficiencies have a way of continually creeping back into the closing process. Consequently, it is necessary to follow an ongoing improvement process to at least keep the close from backsliding and preferably to achieve a continually faster close.

ONGOING IMPROVEMENT PROCESS

One of the most important techniques for improving the closing process is to write down all problems or perceived inefficiencies that occur during the closing process, *no matter how minor they may appear to be*, and discuss them with the closing team prior to the next close. Examples of possible problem areas are:

- Reversing journal entries that were not set to automatically reverse
- Recurring entries that do not stop, because no termination date was set
- Significant expenses that were not accrued
- Incorrect expense accruals
- Incorrect cutoff in the receiving area
- Incorrect month-end billings
- Delays caused by incorrect handoffs of tasks between staff

Of particular importance are problems that recur through multiple closings. By keeping a list of problems and comparing issues to those from prior months, it is easier to see which problem areas are the source of most closing difficulties.

Although it is certainly allowable to review these errors during a formal review meeting, a better alternative is to discuss them over an informal lunch with the closing team. By doing so, it is easier to create a relaxed atmosphere that focuses on problem elimination, rather than on targeting the performance of those people who caused the problems. Also, lunch can be used as a celebration of the most recent successful close. Furthermore, consider conducting the review meeting as soon after the close as possible, rather than waiting even a few days. By doing so, problems are still fresh in everyone's minds, as well as any possible solutions they may have thought of but not written down.

Once a problem is resolved, document the problem and its solution. By doing so, the controller can gradually build up an encyclopedia of issues specific to the company's accounting systems. This is particularly useful as a training tool for new accounting staff, as well as a research document in case problems arise in the future for which solutions were found in the past.

Besides fixing problems, part of the ongoing improvement process involves the analysis of wait times throughout the closing process. This can be done formally by assigning a project team to monitor a typical close to measure the duration of wait times. However, a simpler approach is to have a team meeting right after the close, plot the major closing steps on a white board, and have them estimate where wait times are excessively long. This less formal approach is especially useful when there are still many days in the closing process, so estimated wait times can still be somewhat inaccurate while still providing good information about where the closing team should concentrate its efforts in making wait time reductions.

The elimination of non-value-added (NVA) activities from the closing process can be approached in the same manner as for wait time analysis. This is an especially fruitful activity early in the closing improvement process, where stripping out NVA activities can result in rapid declines in the closing interval. Once the initial list of NVAs has been deleted, some NVAs are likely to creep back into the closing process, so schedule an NVA review thereafter at relatively lengthy intervals.

The closing team should also consider on a monthly basis the need for any additional automation that will speed the closing process. There are likely to be a great many such opportunities early in the closing project and far fewer after the first year. Nonetheless, an automation review should be included in the closing checklist for every month. Also, when there are multiple automation requests early in the closing process, consider releasing only a few of them to the IT department, so the programmers are not completely buried with work requests. By doing so, automation improvements can be implemented at an orderly and fairly predictable pace. IT managers also appreciate not having a wheelbarrow full of requests dumped on them all at once.

If there are multiple divisions in which company accounting transactions are conducted, it is useful to maintain an ongoing analysis of potential areas of standardization, which can streamline the closing process. Because of the difficulty of coordinating standardization activities across divisions, this action item is usually dealt with on a more formal basis, perhaps as a quarterly or annual project.

Once the project team has completed its post-closing review, document all of the changes that the team has agreed upon, including the assignment of task responsibilities, and distribute the list to the team. It may be necessary to follow up on the assigned tasks after a few days, to ensure that changes will be implemented prior to the next close. Also, it is likely that the closing activities checklist will vary a fair amount during the first few months of improvements, so remember to issue a revised closing checklist prior to each month-end.

Finally, even though this may seem like an excessive level of documentation, try to revise the accounting procedures manual on at least a semiannual basis, so it stays in sync with any changes the closing team has made throughout the review process. This frequency can probably be longer if there is a high level of experience within the accounting department and more frequently if there is considerable turnover—newer and less experienced employees require more training, which in turn calls for a more up-to-date procedures manual.

IMPROVEMENT MEASUREMENTS

The simplest approach to measuring the closing process is simply determining the number of days and hours it takes to release financial statements—that is the primary focus of this book. However, once the closing interval declines to just a few days or even hours, it is useful to measure the closing performance in more detail, with an eye to finding areas in which there are still opportunities for improvement. Some possible measurements to consider are:

- *Ratio of adjusting entries to total journal entries during the closing period.* Ideally, if an accounting system has been set up to generate minimal transaction errors, few adjusting entries should be needed. Thus, a high proportion of adjusting entries is a clear indicator of issues with transaction errors.

- *Number of errors found during financial statement review.* A variation on the last measurement is to add up the number of errors found during a general review of the preliminary financial statements.

- *Number of intercompany transactions to reverse.* If there are many intercompany transactions to be eliminated as part of the close, consider adding them up to gain a general understanding of the impact of this activity on the close.

- *Break down time requirements by closing activity.* A common approach is to break down the closing process into discrete pieces and measure the duration of each one, which can be used to target improvement activities in the longest areas. Some subsets of the closing process worth measuring are:

  o Time to obtain division results by division

  o Time to complete payroll close

  o Time to complete invoicing close

  o Time to complete payables close

  o Time to complete inventory close

  o Time to complete cash processing close

  o Time to complete management reports

SUMMARY

In the author's experience, there is no such thing as an entirely stable process—it is either constantly improving or degrading. This principle certainly applies to the closing process, so one should continually review it and make incremental improvements. However, this concept should not be taken so far that the closing team is buried with close-related projects for days after a month-end close has been completed. Instead, consider a measured approach to ongoing improvements, where the closing team allocates a certain number of hours to improvement projects each month and no more. This will allow for the spreading of enhancement work over many months, at a reasonable pace that does not interfere with other work going on within the accounting department.

Appendix A

Comprehensive Closing Checklist

PRIOR TO MONTH-END

- ❒ Review and correct subledger transactions throughout the month
- ❒ Complete the bank reconciliation every day
- ❒ Review uncashed checks
- ❒ Review journal entries:
    - ❒ Verify materiality
    - ❒ Standardize
    - ❒ Convert to recurring entries
- ❒ Update inventory obsolescence reserve
- ❒ Determine the lower of cost or market
- ❒ Calculate overhead allocation bases
- ❒ Bill recurring invoices
- ❒ Conduct a preliminary comparison of the shipping log to invoices issued
- ❒ Review preliminary rebillable expenses
- ❒ Update the bad debt reserve
- ❒ Review preliminary billable hours
- ❒ Accrue interest expense
- ❒ Determine pension plan funding
- ❒ Determine flexible spending account funding

❐ Accrue unpaid wages

❐ Accrue unused vacation time

❐ Accrue travel expenses

❐ Reconcile asset and liability accounts

❐ Update the fixed assets register

❐ Calculate depreciation

❐ Compile preliminary commissions

❐ Review financial statements for errors

❐ Complete selected financial reports in advance

DURING CORE CLOSING PERIOD

❐ Ensure inventory cutoff

❐ Complete all employee/contractor time records

❐ Count and value inventory

❐ Enter late supplier invoices

❐ Complete month-end invoicing

❐ Accrue revenue for unbilled jobs

❐ Accrue commissions on month-end invoicing

❐ Accrue royalties on monthly revenue

❐ Convert division results to reporting currency

❐ Map division results to corporate chart of accounts

❐ Eliminate intercompany transactions

❐ Create and analyze preliminary financial statements

❐ Adjust errors at corporate and division levels

❐ Accrue income tax liability

❐ Finalize and issue financial statements

DEFERRED BEYOND CORE CLOSING PERIOD

❐ Defer the mailing of invoices

❐ Defer the invoicing of rebillable expenses

❐ Complete bank reconciliation based on final bank statement

❏ Calculate and review closing metrics

❏ Determine improvement targets for next month

❏ Initiate programming changes for further improvements

❏ Review accounting systems for standardization opportunities

❏ Update closing procedures

The following additional steps are required for a company issuing quarterly 10-Q or annual 10-K reports to the Securities and Exchange Commission (SEC), which occurs after the financial statements have been completed:

PRIOR TO MONTH-END

❏ Complete portions of SEC- and GAAP-required disclosures

DURING CORE CLOSING PERIOD

❏ Write 10-Q/10-K report

❏ Double-check contents of the 10-Q/10-K report

❏ Complete remaining SEC- and GAAP-required disclosures

❏ Prepare supporting documentation for footnotes and disclosures

❏ Prepare analytics and assemble documents requested by auditors

❏ Obtain legal review of 10-Q/10-K

❏ Obtain officer certifications of 10-Q/10-K

❏ Obtain audit committee approval of 10-Q/10-K

❏ Prepare report for submission to the SEC

❏ Obtain final approval from auditors for filing

❏ File the report with the SEC's EDGAR system

Appendix B

Fast Close Policies and Procedures*

Appendix A contained a list of the closing activities one should normally complete, split into the periods prior to month-end, during the core closing period, and those deferred beyond the core closing period. That list is intended for a single person who is responsible for the entire closing process. This appendix is intended for a larger closing team and breaks down the closing activities into more detail by job position. The first procedure is a single large one for the controller to review each day, revealing which person on the team should be engaged in which activity. The following procedures are broken down by individual position and are provided in more detail and intended for use by specific individuals on the closing team.

---

*The procedure examples in this appendix have been adapted with permission from Chapter 6 of Bragg, *Design & Maintenance of Accounting Manuals*, 4th Edition. (Hoboken, NJ: John Wiley & Sons, Inc., 2003).

Policy/Procedure Statement	Retrieval No.: 10-250
Subject: Period-End Activities	Issue Date: 4/30/05
	Supersedes: N/A

Days from Month-End	Responsibility	Task Description
Daily	General ledger accountant	• Review and correct subledger transactions throughout the month. • Complete the bank reconciliation every day.
−4	General ledger accountant	• Review journal entries, for materiality, standardization opportunities, and possible conversion to recurring entries. • Review uncashed checks.
−4	Cost accountant	• Update the inventory obsolescence reserve. • Determine the lower of cost or market valuation. • Calculate overhead allocation bases.
−2	Accounts receivable clerk	• Bill recurring invoices.
−1	Accounts receivable clerk	• Conduct a preliminary comparison of the shipping log to invoices issued. • Update the bad debt reserve.
−1	Accounts payable clerk	• Review preliminary rebillable expenses. • Accrue travel expenses.
−1	Payroll clerk	• Review preliminary billable hours. • Determine pension plan funding. • Determine flexible spending account funding. • Accrue unpaid wages. • Accrue unused vacation time. • Compile preliminary commissions.
−1	General ledger clerk	• Accrue interest expense. • Reconcile asset and liability accounts. • Review financial statements for errors.
−1	Fixed assets clerk	• Update the fixed assets register. • Calculate depreciation.

−1	Financial analyst	• Complete selected financial reports in advance.
0	Cost accountant	• Ensure inventory cutoff. • Count and value inventory.
0	Payroll clerk	• Complete all employee/contractor time records. • Accrue commissions on month-end invoicing.
0	Accounts payable clerk	• Enter late supplier invoices. • Accrue royalties on monthly revenue.
0	Accounts receivable clerk	• Complete month-end invoicing. • Accrue revenue for unbilled jobs.
0	General ledger clerk	• Convert division results to reporting currency. • Map division results to corporate chart of accounts. • Eliminate intercompany transactions. • Adjust errors at corporate and division levels. • Accrue income tax liability.
0	Financial analyst	• Create and analyze preliminary financial statements. • Finalize and issue financial statements.
+1	Accounts receivable clerk	• Issue deferred invoice mailings. • Issue deferred rebillable expense invoices.
+2	Financial analyst	• Calculate and review closing metrics.
+2	Controller	• Determine improvement targets for next month. • Initiate programming changes for further improvements. • Review accounting systems for standardization opportunities. • Update closing procedures.
+3	General ledger clerk	• Complete bank reconciliations based on final bank statements.

Policy/Procedure Statement	Retrieval No.: 10-251
Subject: Accounts Payable Closing Activities	Issue Date: 4/30/05
	Supersedes: N/A

Days from Month-End	Task Description
−1	• *Review preliminary rebillable expenses.* Go to the rebillable expenses account in the general ledger and verify that expense reports have been received for all weeks in which travel has been approved. If expense reports have not been recorded, contact employees and request that the expense reports be sent to the accounting department at once. • *Accrue travel expenses.* Have the travel department forward a list of employees who have gone on approved trips during the month, including the airfare costs as processed by the travel department. Based on the departure and return dates on these airfares, calculate per-diem lodging and meals charges. Calculate the travel expense accrual based on this information, less the amount of any expense reports received from employees.
0	• *Enter late supplier invoices.* If supplier invoices arrive during the core closing period and they have not already been accrued, enter them as expenses in the reporting period. • *Accrue royalties on monthly revenue.* Review the royalty checklist to verify the amount of royalty expense to record based on billed revenues. Record this as an account payable in the reporting period.

Policy/Procedure Statement	Retrieval No.: 10-252
Subject: Accounts Receivable Closing Activities	Issue Date: 4/30/05
	Supersedes: N/A

Days from Month-End	Task Description
−2	• *Bill recurring invoices.* Print the recurring invoices report from the subscription database and forward it to the sales manager for review and approval. Once returned, make any changes noted by the sales manager. Then set the accounting system's database date to the next reporting period and print the recurring invoices. Reset the system date to the current reporting period. Mail the invoices to customers.
−1	• *Conduct a preliminary review of the shipping log to invoices issued.* Print the invoices register and compare it to a copy of the shipping log, crossing off invoiced shipments from the shipping log. If there are any remaining shipments on the shipping log after all invoices have been accounted for, request a copy of the bill of lading and investigate why no invoice was issued. Report findings to the controller.
	• *Update the bad debt reserve.* Discuss the accounts receivable aging with the credit manager, highlighting prospective collection problems with newer invoices, as well as the status of older unpaid ones. Adjust the bad debt reserve to reflect the anticipated bad debts. As a cross-check, stratify the aging report by 30-day time bucket and apply the historical bad debt loss rate to each bucket. Compare the result to the bad debt reserve and adjust the reserve accordingly.
0	• *Complete month-end invoicing.* Verify that all shipments have been made and that employees whose hours are billable have completed their entries of hours worked into the timekeeping system. Process invoices. Forward them to another clerk for error checks, and revise as necessary. Set the invoices aside for later mailing.
	• *Accrue revenue for unbilled jobs.* If there are jobs for which hours have been worked but no invoice is to be issued, summarize the billable rates and hours to determine the amount that would have been billed. Adjust this amount downward if it would exceed any fixed billable total for the job, and create a journal entry to record the accrued revenue.
+1	• *Issue deferred invoice mailings.* If invoices were run during the core closing period and not mailed, mail them now.
	• *Issue deferred rebillable expense invoices.* If employee expense reports that are rebillable arrive after the close has been completed, reopen the old accounting period and enter the expense reports in the rebillable asset account. Then reopen the affected invoices, add the expense reports to them, and reprint the invoices. Review the invoices for errors and then mail them.

Policy/Procedure Statement	Retrieval No.: 10-253
Subject: Controller Closing Activities	Issue Date: 4/30/05
	Supersedes: N/A

Days from Month-End	Task Description
−4	• *Review closing schedule and distribute to staff.* Print a different schedule for each staff person, depending on the tasks required of each person. Then distribute the schedules in person and go over with the recipients any changes from the previous closing process.
+2	• *Determine improvement targets for next month.* Meet with the closing team to determine where errors were made during the current close, as well as to review a process flow and see where additional time can be stripped out of the closing process. Agree on the top few items in need of change, and who will work on them prior to the next close. Document these changes in a memo and distribute it to the closing team. • *Initiate programming changes for further improvements.* If programming changes were considered necessary by the closing team, prepare a written request and meet with the IT manager to discuss it. Obtain an anticipated completion date and communicate this information back to the closing team. • *Review accounting systems for standardization opportunities.* Determine if there are variations in the manner in which transactions are being completed, and formulate ways to standardize them. • *Update closing procedures.* Access the soft copy of the accounting procedures manual and update it based on any changes resulting from the closing team's recommendations. E-mail the report to the accounting department, with commentary as necessary.

Policy/Procedure Statement	Retrieval No.: 10-254
Subject: Cost Accountant Closing Activities	Issue Date: 4/30/05 Supersedes: N/A

Days from Month-End	Task Description
−4	• *Update the inventory obsolescence reserve.* Print the "where used" report to spot any unused inventory that is no longer included in any bills of materials. Meet with the Materials Review Board to review these items and determine their disposition. Adjust the inventory obsolescence reserve based on this information. • *Determine the lower of cost or market valuation.* Obtain a listing of raw material market prices from the purchasing department and compare these prices to the costs at which they are recorded for in-house inventory items. If the recorded cost exceeds market value, prepare a journal entry that writes down their value to market. Forward the entry to the controller for review and approval. • *Calculate overhead allocation bases.* Verify with the controller what activities are being used as allocation bases, and then compile the latest activity information for these items. Compare the activity totals to the totals from the last reporting period for consistency, and report any anomalies exceeding 15% to the controller.
0	• *Ensure inventory cutoff.* Send an e-mail to the receiving manager, verifying that inventory receipts will be recorded in the proper accounting period. Conduct a spotcheck of receiving records on the morning of the core closing period to ensure that this is the case. • *Count and value inventory.* If cycle counts of the inventory reveal accuracy levels exceeding 95%, no formal month-end inventory count is necessary—instead, print the inventory report, calculate metrics, and compare the results to the metrics from the prior three periods. If they are similar, close the inventory module. If not, conduct further investigation into significant changes.

Policy/Procedure Statement	Retrieval No.: 10-255
Subject: Financial Analysis Closing Activities	Issue Date: 4/30/05 Supersedes: N/A

Days from Month-End	Task Description
−1	• *Complete selected financial reports in advance.* Create a boilerplate format for the controller's discussion page. Also update any information in the accompanying footnotes. If Excel spreadsheets are attached, verify that formulas are correct. If any operating information can be obtained prior to month-end, record this information in the financial reports.
0	• *Create and analyze preliminary financial statements.* Print the income statement and balance sheet, as well as the income statement for each division. Calculate metrics, search for anomalies, and investigate them as necessary. • *Finalize and issue financial statements.* Print the adjusted financial statements and forward them to the controller for approval. Then print them, carry forward information into accompanying footnotes and spreadsheets as necessary, and convert to PDF format for electronic distribution to recipients.
+2	• *Calculate and review closing metrics.* Calculate the total duration of the close, durations by functional area, and durations by division. Forward this information to the controller.

Policy/Procedure Statement	Retrieval No.: 10-256
Subject: Fixed Assets Closing Activities	Issue Date: 4/30/05
	Supersedes: N/A

Days from Month-End	Task Description
−1	• *Update the fixed assets register.* Ensure that all accounts payable have been recorded in the current accounting period. Then print the general ledger to see what assets have been added during the period. Transfer this information to the fixed assets register and store supporting purchase documentation in the fixed assets binder, sorted by asset type. • *Calculate depreciation.* Print the depreciation report in the fixed assets register. Compare the depreciation expense in this report to the recurring depreciation entry, and adjust the recurring entry to match the report.

Days from Month-End	Task Description
Daily	• *Review and correct subledger transactions throughout the month.* Scan the subledger transactions for obvious anomalies in terms of the size of transactions or the accounts to which they are charged, and investigate as necessary. • *Complete the bank reconciliation every day.* Access Internet-based bank records and reconcile this information for every bank account, creating adjusting entries as necessary.
−4	• *Review journal entries for materiality, standardization opportunities, and possible conversion to recurring entries.* This is intended to be a quick scan of the standard journal entry package to see if any additional efficiencies can be achieved. • *Review uncashed checks.* Print the uncashed checks report and contact recipients if checks sent to them are more than 60 days old.
−1	• *Accrue interest expense.* Calculate the number of days over which debt has been outstanding during the month, multiply it by the daily interest rate, and record the monthly interest expense based on this information. • *Reconcile asset and liability accounts.* Update the manual schedules of the contents of all asset and liability accounts. • *Review financial statements for errors.* Print all financial statements and compare them to the statements from the prior period, looking for anomalies. Investigate and correct as necessary. Report significant errors to the controller.
0	• *Convert division results to reporting currency.* Verify that the currency valuations in the currency conversion table match currency rates at month-end, and process the currency conversion. • *Map division results to corporate chart of accounts.* Verify that no chart of account changes have occurred during the month, and verify that the control totals submitted by the divisional accounting departments match the mapped totals recorded by the consolidation software. If not, search for unmapped accounts and correct as necessary. • *Eliminate intercompany transactions.* Print the intercompany transactions report and create an adjusting entry based on this information. • *Adjust errors at corporate and division levels.* If errors are noted in the corporate-level financial statements, be sure to communicate the adjusting entries back to the divisional accounting staffs. • *Accrue income tax liability.* Obtain the income tax accrual from the corporate tax manager and record the entry.
+3	• *Complete bank reconciliations based on final bank statements.* Once printed bank statements are received from the bank, verify that these match the Internet-based statements already used, and file the statements.

Policy/Procedure Statement	Retrieval No.: 10-258
Subject: Payroll Closing Activities	Issue Date: 4/30/05
	Supersedes: N/A

Days from Month-End	Task Description
−1	• *Review preliminary billable hours.* Print the timekeeping report and see who has not recorded hours for the billing period. Send them reminder messages to do so.
	• *Determine pension plan funding.* Based on the monthly payroll reports, determine the amount of employee 401k deductions that must be shifted to the independent 401k provider, and record this cash transfer.
	• *Determine flexible spending account (FSA) funding.* Based on the monthly payroll reports, determine the amount of employee FSA deductions that must be shifted to the FSA administration company, and record this cash transfer.
	• *Accrue unpaid wages.* Compile unpaid hours worked for hourly employees and multiply these hours by standard hourly rates to arrive at the unpaid wages accrual.
	• *Accrue unused vacation time.* Update the unused vacation time spreadsheet with any pay rate changes, additional accrued vacation time, and used vacation time. Compare the result to the accrued vacation expense balance, and adjust the balance as necessary.
0	• *Complete all employee/contractor time records.* Contact all employees and contractors who have not completed their prior-month time records, and have them do so at once.
	• *Accrue commissions on month-end invoicing.* Calculate commissions based on final invoicing. Forward the calculations to the sales manager for review, and accrue the amount of the commissions.

Appendix C

Soft Close Checklist

Although this book has been entirely concerned with the standard fast close, there are occasions when a soft close might be an acceptable alternative. If so, the following checklist can be used instead of the one presented in Appendix A. The presentation is the same as the one shown in Appendix A, except that those tasks not required for a soft close have been shifted to a "Deleted Activities" section at the end of the appendix.

It is immediately obvious that most closing tasks have been removed from the soft close list. The removal is based on the following assumptions:

- Inventory accuracy is high enough to avoid a physical count.

- Inventory and bad debt reserves are being supplemented with consistent recurring journal entries every month, and so require no additional adjustment during soft close months.

- All accrued expenses are relatively consistent from month to month, and so require no special review during soft close months.

- There is little activity in the asset and liability accounts, so that infrequent reconciliations are sufficient.

- The depreciation expense will be updated at least quarterly with new information about asset acquisitions and sales.

- The income tax liability will be updated on a quarterly basis, in time for tax payments to the government.

The result of deleting so many closing steps is a very short closing list that concentrates on month-end billings and related commission calculations (which are presumably paid every month and so must be calculated anyway). The list is as follows:

PRIOR TO MONTH-END

❏ Review and correct subledger transactions throughout the month

❏ Complete the bank reconciliation every day

❏ Bill recurring invoices

❏ Conduct a preliminary comparison of the shipping log to invoices issued

❏ Review preliminary rebillable expenses

❏ Review preliminary billable hours

❏ Compile preliminary commissions

❏ Review financial statements for errors

DURING CORE CLOSING PERIOD

❏ Complete all employee/contractor time records

❏ Enter late supplier invoices

❏ Complete month-end invoicing

❏ Accrue commissions on month-end invoicing

❏ Convert division results to reporting currency

❏ Map division results to corporate chart of accounts

❏ Create and analyze preliminary financial statements

❏ Adjust errors at corporate and division levels

❏ Finalize and issue financial statements

DEFERRED BEYOND CORE CLOSING PERIOD

❏ Defer the mailing of invoices

❏ Defer the invoicing of rebillable expenses

❏ Complete bank reconciliation based on final bank statement

DELETED ACTIVITIES

❏ Review uncashed checks

❏ Review journal entries:

    ❏ Verify materiality

❒ Standardize

❒ Convert to recurring entries

❒ Update inventory obsolescence reserve

❒ Determine the lower of cost or market

❒ Calculate overhead allocation bases

❒ Update the bad debt reserve

❒ Accrue interest expense

❒ Determine pension plan funding

❒ Determine flexible spending account funding

❒ Accrue unpaid wages

❒ Accrue unused vacation time

❒ Accrue travel expenses

❒ Reconcile asset and liability accounts

❒ Update the fixed assets register

❒ Calculate depreciation

❒ Complete selected financial reports in advance

❒ Ensure inventory cutoff

❒ Count and value inventory

❒ Accrue revenue for unbilled jobs

❒ Accrue royalties on monthly revenue

❒ Eliminate intercompany transactions

❒ Accrue income tax liability

❒ Calculate and review closing metrics

❒ Determine improvement targets for next month

❒ Initiate programming changes for further improvements

❒ Review accounting systems for standardization opportunities

❒ Update closing procedures

Appendix D

Year-End Close Checklist

The closing process can also be compressed at year-end, although several audit- and payroll-related issues require additional effort before the process can be completed. The following procedure is the same as the summary-level one shown in Appendix B, but it includes all additional year-end activities. Of special interest is that no year-end audit activities should impinge on the core closing period, with the possible exception of a physical inventory count. However, if the auditors test inventory controls and conduct test counts in advance (as assumed in this procedure), then no additional counting is required beyond the usual level required for the month-end close.

Policy/Procedure Statement	Retrieval No.: 10-260
Subject: Year-End Closing Activities	Issue Date: 4/30/05
	Supersedes: N/A

Days from Month-End	Responsibility	Task Description
Daily	General ledger accountant	• Review and correct subledger transactions throughout the month. • Complete the bank reconciliation every day.
−5	Controller	• Assist the auditors in conducting a controls review. • Assist the auditors in planning their review of the physical inventory count.
−4	General ledger accountant	• Review journal entries, for materiality, standardization opportunities, and possible conversion to recurring entries. • Review uncashed checks.
−4	Cost accountant	• Update the inventory obsolescence reserve. • Determine the lower of cost or market valuation. • Calculate overhead allocation bases. • Document the overhead allocation methodology and set aside for the auditors. • Conduct an annual update of standard costs in bills of materials to reflect actual costs. • Audit the scrap rates in bills of materials and adjust to match actual scrap rates.
−2	Accounts receivable clerk	• Bill recurring invoices.
−1	Accounts receivable clerk	• Conduct a preliminary comparison of the shipping log to invoices issued. • Update the bad debt reserve.
−1	Accounts payable clerk	• Review preliminary rebillable expenses. • Accrue travel expenses.
−1	Payroll clerk	• Review preliminary billable hours. • Determine pension plan funding. • Determine flexible spending account funding. • Accrue unpaid wages. • Accrue unused vacation time. • Compile preliminary commissions. • If at calendar year-end, prepare payroll checks including as recognized employee income the amount of company-paid life insurance exceeding the federally mandated maximum value.

−1	General ledger clerk	• Accrue interest expense. • Reconcile asset and liability accounts. • Review financial statements for errors.
−1	Fixed assets clerk	• Update the fixed assets register. • Calculate depreciation.
−1	Financial analyst	• Complete selected financial reports in advance.
0	Cost accountant	• Ensure inventory cutoff. • Count and value inventory.
0	Payroll clerk	• Complete all employee/contractor time records. • Accrue commissions on month-end invoicing.
0	Accounts payable clerk	• Enter late supplier invoices. • Accrue royalties on monthly revenue.
0	Accounts receivable clerk	• Complete month-end invoicing. • Accrue revenue for unbilled jobs.
0	General ledger clerk	• Convert division results to reporting currency. • Map division results to corporate chart of accounts. • Eliminate intercompany transactions. • Adjust errors at corporate and division levels. • Accrue income tax liability.
0	Financial analyst	• Create and analyze preliminary financial statements. • Finalize and issue financial statements.
+1	Accounts payable clerk	• Print the accounts payable listing for year-end and set aside for the auditors. • Compile all legal invoices for the year and set aside for the auditors.
+1	Accounts receivable clerk	• Issue deferred invoice mailings. • Issue deferred rebillable expense invoices. • Print the year-end aged accounts receivable report and set aside for the auditors. • Assist the auditors in sending receivable confirmations to customers.
+1	Fixed assets clerk	• Calculate depreciation as per tax regulations, and set aside for the auditors.
+1	Payroll clerk	• Prepare a listing of employees and their annual pay, and set aside for the auditors.
+2	Financial analyst	• Calculate and review closing metrics.

| +2 | Controller | • Determine improvement targets for next month.
• Initiate programming changes for further improvements.
• Review accounting systems for standardization opportunities.
• Update closing procedures.
• Compile a list of all current contracts, with attached contract copies, and set aside for the auditors.
• Assist auditors in sending legal opinion letters to company lawyers. |
| +3 | General ledger clerk | • Complete bank reconciliations based on final bank statements.
• Update detailed schedules for all balance sheet accounts and set aside for the auditors. |

Index